lonely planet

OFFSEASON

SARAH BAXTER & PAUL BLOOMFIELD

Anghiari, a medieval town in Tuscany

Contents

Introduction

● Aaah, the bliss of pinpointing the secret travel sweet spot. We found it hiking the Corfu Trail in spring: we were doused in sunshine, mercury zooming above 20°C (68°F). Wildflowers and herbs bloomed in kaleidoscopic colours and spritzed the breeze. Confetti-storms of butterflies danced around our feet. Tourists, though? Nada, pretty much. Late April in the northernmost of Greece's Ionian Islands blessed us with everything we could want – and subtracted most of what we didn't.

True, some tavernas were still shuttered, and the turquoise Mediterranean was... invigorating, let's say, but we had that pellucid sea and those spectacular footpaths largely to ourselves. No need for restaurant reservations: walk-ins were easy. And the vibe was near-horizontal chilled. In short, it was the perfect time to dodge the hordes.

In our age of overtourism, travelling out of season should be a no-brainer. Prices can be lower, accommodation easier to find, crowds thinner. You might bag a bargain safari in Africa, snag last-minute tickets for epic must-sees like Machu Picchu, or discover new facets of familiar destinations – ski resorts in summer, say, or popular European cities in winter when you can enjoy bucket-list sights sans the masses.

Of course, there's no point getting drenched or freezing in the brutal cold if it's just going to be miserable. Though rainforest can be most alluring in, well, the rain, some places are simply no-go zones in the wrong months – heading to Antarctica in July would be madness, if it were even possible. But it can pay to think outside the season, even by just a little. Optimal moments often come in shoulder months, those windows before or after the peak when hotels, lodges, restaurants and tour operators are begging for your business.

The trick is knowing how to find each destination's decisive moment – and it's not as simple as checking the weather forecast. Peak season doesn't always mean summer or snowfall. Some places are busiest when rains are heaviest, because that's when family holidays are planned, or when festivals buzz to the max. So how do you get the timing just right?

Never fear – in these pages you'll find 100 ideas for your next off-season adventure. They're organised by month, but most suggestions cover longer periods – so a destination we've tipped for May might also be great in April or June.

Whenever you want to travel, whatever you like to do, wherever you hope to go, we've got you covered.

—Sarah Baxter & Paul Bloomfield

Left: Paradise Bay, Antarctica **Opposite:** Cenote Ik Kil, Yucatán, Mexico

Sydney Opera House, Botanic Gardens and harbour, New South Wales

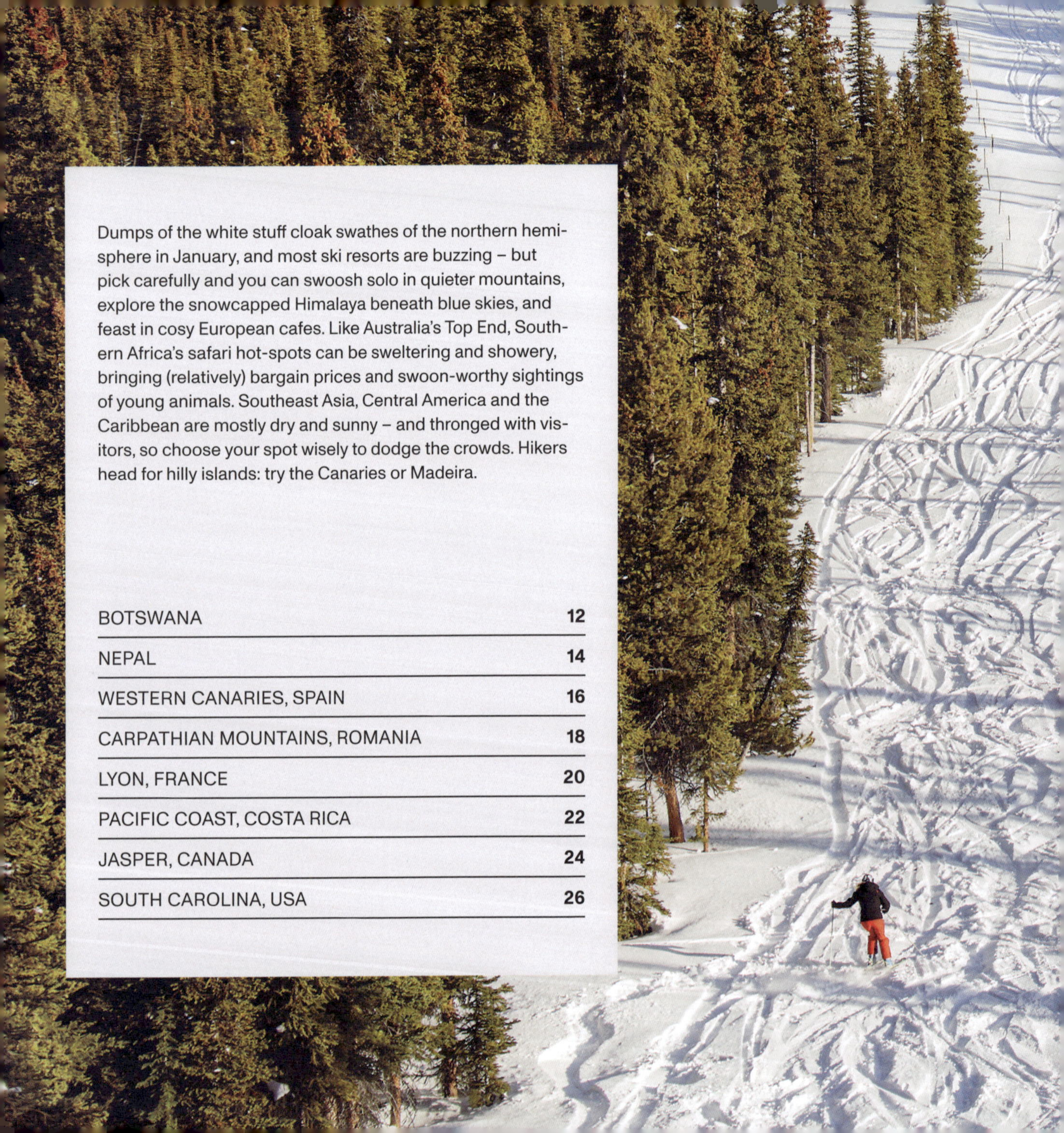

Dumps of the white stuff cloak swathes of the northern hemisphere in January, and most ski resorts are buzzing – but pick carefully and you can swoosh solo in quieter mountains, explore the snowcapped Himalaya beneath blue skies, and feast in cosy European cafes. Like Australia's Top End, Southern Africa's safari hot-spots can be sweltering and showery, bringing (relatively) bargain prices and swoon-worthy sightings of young animals. Southeast Asia, Central America and the Caribbean are mostly dry and sunny – and thronged with visitors, so choose your spot wisely to dodge the crowds. Hikers head for hilly islands: try the Canaries or Madeira.

JANUARY

Botswana

DECEMBER–MARCH

GREEN DREAMS

● Wildlife watching goes free-range in southern Africa's most deluxe and desirable destination. No fences here – in Botswana, mammoth herds of elephants, cunning lion prides and crashes (true story) of rhinos roam at will. This is Africa for aficionados, promising diverse landscapes as well as some of the planet's most incredible herbivore migrations, astonishing predator encounters...and astounding prices.

Newsflash: Botswana ain't cheap. That's no accident, it's a strategy to dodge the pitfalls of mass tourism. But there are ways of saving your bucks. Most safari-goers plump for prime time – June to October, when temperatures and rainfall are lower but Okavango Delta water levels higher. But in 'green season' it's not just the rain that falls, so do visitor numbers and prices at those kerching camps. Pick the right spot and you'll still experience next-level wildlife viewing and unique visual spectacles – zingy pink flamingos reflected in the flooded Makgadikgadi Pans, say.

And don't forget the sunscreen. You'll enjoy plenty of dry, sunny days, with short, sharp showers (and sometimes dramatic thunderstorms) mostly arriving late afternoon or evening, painting the land green with lush foliage. New life is burgeoning all around, in fact: the emerald bush is alive with breeding birds, and many herbivores are giving birth and raising young.

Left: Okavango Delta Opposite: Lilac-breasted roller, Chobe National Park

EXPERIENCES

STALK PREDATORS: Watch lions, leopards and cheetahs hunt prey in Chobe National Park or Moremi Game Reserve.

BOOST YOUR BIRDING: Thrill to an alfresco aviary of breeding migrant birds – binoculars ready!

TAKE A CRÈCHE COURSE: Stacks of species give birth this month, so keep eyes peeled for young animals (and the hungry creatures that hunt them) in the Kalahari and elsewhere.

TRACK THE TREK: Take in Africa's longest terrestrial mammal migration: huge herds of zebra rumbling across Nxai and Makgadikgadi Pans.

NEED TO KNOW

Botswana's hot and humid in January – prep for over 30°C (86°F). Though it's the rainy summer season, Okavango Delta waters are typically low now, and wildlife disperses: for max animal magic, head for its south and east flanks, or go large at Chief's Island for Big Five action (with prices to match, albeit lower than at the winter peak).

Nepal

DECEMBER–FEBRUARY

COOLER CULTURE

● In the market for insulation? Come to Nepal's capital, where a dizzying selection of colourful knitted woollen gloves, socks and hats are snapped up by visitors passing through en route to trek the Himalaya – and by those who just come to explore the country in winter. Yup, it's cold: nighttime temperatures in Kathmandu, sitting at about 1500m (4921ft) altitude, duck down towards freezing in January. No surprise, then, that high-level treks tend not to run in the depths of winter (between mid-December and February), and tourist numbers everywhere thin out, damping down prices.

Yet if your ambitions don't run to cloud-shrouded passes, Nepal's nigh perfect now. Sure, you'll want to huddle under blankets after sundown, but days are sunny and mild, ideal for exploring medieval palaces and ancient Buddhist and Hindu temples around the Kathmandu Valley. Now's also the season to roam the perky lakeside town of Pokhara; perched at about 800m (2625ft), it's that bit warmer, and has easy access to paths through foothills affording spectacular views of the Annapurna Range.

And Nepal's not all mountains: head south to the steaming lowland Terai region and Chitwan National Park (or quieter Bardia), where tall elephant grass is cut in late January, making it easier to spot the wildest life.

EXPERIENCES

DISCOVER SACRED SITES: Roam the medieval streets of historic Bhaktapur, monkey-thronged Swayambhunath and the vast Buddhist stupa of Boudhanath (remember to walk clockwise).

WATCH WILDLIFE: Delve into the forests of Chitwan National Park, watching for rhinos, deer, monkeys and, if you're lucky, Royal Bengal tigers.

HIKE THE HILLS: Hit the trails from Pokhara to enjoy extraordinary views of the Annapurna at Sarangkot, a lovely day-hike away; or tackle a more challenging trek, perhaps to Poon Hill.

SHOP AND EAT AROUND KATHMANDU: Nepal's rapidly expanding capital is an enthralling (if sometimes infuriating) city to explore.

NEED TO KNOW

Nepalese tourist visas can be bought on arrival at Kathmandu Airport, but queues are often long, so it can be more convenient to apply in advance through the consulate in your home country. Thamel is the capital's most popular tourist district, convenient for sights and services but hectic – consider a base in Patan or even Boudhanath for a more mellow experience.

Left, from top: Rhino, Chitwan National Park; Swayambhunath Stupa, Kathmandu Valley **Opposite:** Annapurna Range

Western Canaries, Spain

NOVEMBER–FEBRUARY

MILD BUT OFFBEAT

● The seven Atlantic-scattered Canary Islands might just be blessed with the world's best weather: blue skies, scant rain and warm-to-hot temperatures year-round. This results in two peak seasons – traditional high summer, when beach-lovers want to bake on the islands' ink-black and golden sands, and the mild winter months, when northern Europeans are desperate for sunshine. However, the archipelago's lusher western isles – La Palma, El Hierro, La Gomera – see a fraction of the tourists that descend on Lanzarote and Tenerife at any time of year, so it can feel off-season even when the weather is good and the offer enticing.

This applies particularly to tiny, remote El Hierro (a UNESCO Biosphere Reserve) and verdant La Gomera, known as Isla Mágica (Magical Island). Neither have international airports; both remain pretty much crowd-free. They are also excellent for winter hiking, offering around eight hours of sunshine a day, average highs of around 22°C (72°F), and plenty of tempting trails. On La Gomera you can walk into plummeting barranca (deep gorges), along volcanic ridges and through rare laurel forests that drip with moss. El Hierro is like another planet, with routes leading along the basalt-edged coast and into an interior of both lunar-like strangeness and subtropical abundance.

EXPERIENCES

APPRECIATE MARINE LIFE: Whales and dolphins can be seen year-round (boat tours run from La Gomera), while La Restinga – an underwater lava-scape at El Hierro's southern tip – is the archipelago's finest scuba site.

EXPLORE PARQUE NACIONAL DE GARAJONAY: La Gomera's trekking treasure, where trails wend amid ancient rainforest-like terrain, home to many endemic species.

SOAK UP LOCAL LIFE: Experience authentic Canarios hospitality, from the bright-painted streets of San Sebastián (La Gomera's tiny capital) to the unspoilt villages of El Hierro.

STARGAZE: La Palma is a designated Starlight Reserve, with superlative dark skies.

NEED TO KNOW

Ferries link Tenerife to La Gomera (one hour) and El Hierro (two hours). There are also interisland flights, and La Palma has an international airport. These three are the wettest islands in the Canaries, with January and February the rainiest months, but the weather is still pleasant. The islands' mountainous interiors may be misty and significantly cooler – warm layers and waterproofs are advised.

Left, from top: La Gomera; Charco Azul, a natural pool in San Andrés y Sauces **Opposite:** San Sebastián, La Gomera

JANUARY–FEBRUARY

CHILLS AND THRILLS

Carpathian Mountains, Romania

● 'Children of the night – what music they make...' so said Bram Stoker's Dracula as he listened to a pack of howling wolves. Now is when these wolves howl their eerie songs, with lynx providing harmonies as both species scour the mountains in search of mates. Around 10% – some 3000 – of Europe's grey wolves prowl the central Carpathians.

Summer is when the vampire-hunting masses flock to Bran Castle and the medieval marvels of Brasov, Sighisoara and Sibiu. But in January, in the snowy depths of winter when temperatures rarely peak above freezing, sharp-fanged creatures roam Transylvania's wilder expanses – especially wildlife hotspot Piatra Craiului National Parl – in relative peace.

But don't be a snowflake: wrap up well against the icy bite and drink in dramatic scenery and historic sites beneath a winter-white blanket. In fact, make the most of the chill. Don snowshoes to explore remote trails and historic Saxon villages such as Viscri, seemingly little-changed in centuries. Or book into an igloo at the Hotel of Ice, cradled in the Făgăraș Mountains near Bâlea Lake – significantly cheaper than Sweden's better-known subzero stay. And you can always warm up with a steaming bowl of tarragon-heavy soup or a shot of plus-proofed *pălincă* (plum brandy).

EXPERIENCES

FOLLOW IN WOLVES' PAWPRINTS: From the second half of January, join an expert guide to track wolves from the ancient Transylvanian town of Zărnești.

TASTE HOME LIFE: Bed down in a homestay or small guesthouse to experience traditional village life and food, including hearty soups, farm-fresh cheeses and vegetables.

CAPTURE THE CASTLES: As well as picturesque Bran, popularly (but erroneously) linked with Dracula, other bastions to admire include mighty Râşnov, fang-turreted Corvin and whimsical Peleș.

BRUSH UP ON HISTORY: Explore medieval Saxon villages near Sibiu and Braşov, their churches adorned with magnificent frescoes.

NEED TO KNOW

Bucharest and Sibiu are the handiest airports for exploring Transylvania and the wider Carpathians. Buses from both take about 2½ hours to reach Braşov, the closest major hub to Piatra Craiului National Park. Rural poverty remains a harsh reality in remote regions of Romania; where possible, stay in a traditional family-run guesthouse to help reinvigorate local economies and make real connections with communities.

Left, from top: Romanian cuisine; lynx, Carpathian Mountains **Opposite:** Bran Castle

Lyon, France

NOVEMBER–FEBRUARY

WINTER BELLY-WARMING

● It might be freezing outside, but in France's food capital, every cafe, bistro and *bouchon* (traditional restaurant) is hot, hot, hot inside – even in the depths of winter. With more restaurants per square metre than, well, anywhere in the world, and as the birthplace of nouvelle cuisine, Lyon – sitting pretty at the meeting of the Rhône and Saône rivers – knows how to feed up and warm up travellers who come in the offseason. That's because the city's traditional dishes are a hearty bunch: there are moreish *grattons* (a kind-of Frenchified pork scratching) and battered tripe, doughnut-y *bugnes* and abundant *andouillette* (offal sausages, much less awful than they sound).

Not only that, but across the cobblestone alleys of Vieux-Lyon, Croix-Rousse and the river-hemmed Presqu'île district – between them, a shopper's paradise, perfect for the *soldes d'hiver* (aka January sales) – lie hundreds of *traboules*. These snaking covered passageways, originally built for silk weavers, offer the perfect shelter for grazing at cosy cafes and boutique-hopping away from the elements. And when you're warm inside with a pile of pike dumplings or a big glass of Beaujolais – or even learning to whip up French classics at one of the city's cookery schools – the cold's no issue.

Left: Lyon's Presqu'île district **Opposite:** Lyonnais *andouillette*

EXPERIENCES

GO NUTS: Pink praline is a Lyonnaise speciality. Scoff it in the form of praline pastries, praline roses or blush-coloured *tarte aux pralines*.

EAT AT A BOUCHON: These traditional Lyon bistros are the places for proper Lyonnaise cuisine (but be warned: only 22 are officially certified, but many others call themselves *bouchon* anyway).

THINK BIG: On the central 'island' of Presqu'île, between the Rhône and Saône rivers, the Musée des Confluences has permanent exhibitions covering life, death and everything in between.

WRAP UP FOR A WALK: Tête d'Or (Golden Head) is one of France's biggest urban parks, perfect for a cheek-rosying stroll.

NEED TO KNOW

Time your winter visit for December instead and you'll find bigger crowds but greater sparkle. Lyon's lively Christmas markets run late November to Christmas Eve, while the Fête des Lumières – when creative illuminations dazzle across the city – is held in early December. January and February are better for a ski break: resorts such as Méribel and Courchevel are only a two-hour drive from Lyon.

Pacific Coast, Costa Rica

JANUARY

HIGH-SEASON SWEET SPOT

● Costa Rica is that magical mix of wildness and accessibility, adventure and ease. The Central American nation, known for its rampant nature and 'pura vida' – a carefree, positive outlook – has wow factor, but also the developed infrastructure to deliver the perfect break.

January isn't technically off-season. The country gets busy around Christmas and New Year, then it's straight into peak time, which runs into March – this is when the weather is sunniest and driest. However, there's a little sweet spot in the first few weeks of January, after the festive surge, when things are relatively quiet. Hit that lull and you'll get the best weather but with far fewer people between you and the sloths, monkeys, turtles, whales, volcanoes and beach huts.

The Pacific coast is at its best January to February. Popular parks like super-diverse Manuel Antonio will be busy, but you can avoid the masses on the Península de Nicoya – perfect for chilling on fabulous beaches and catching swell surf. Further south, the Península de Osa is harder to reach, and thus even quieter and wilder. This is where you'll find Parque Nacional Corcovado, a rainforest wonderland occupying almost half of the peninsula, and home to nearly 3% of all the species in the world.

EXPERIENCES

EXPLORE CORCOVADO: Hike a jungle trail for intimate wildlife encounters – potentially monkeys, tapirs, sloths and jaguars (a certified guide is mandatory).

DIVE IN: Isla del Caño, a 40-minute boat ride from Osa's Drake Bay, offers mind-blowing diving and snorkelling amid brain corals, sea plumes and manta rays.

MEET THE TICOS: Seek out the Caminos de Osa, an initiative aiming to boost rural tourism across the peninsula. Experiences include hikes, gold-panning and cacao-farm tours.

GO TO SURF SCHOOL: Learn on the Península de Nicoya's consistent breaks, in spots like lively Tamarindo and relaxed Nosara.

NEED TO KNOW

January is still a peak month, so don't expect bargain prices. For reduced rates, consider wetter May and June, before the summer holiday boom; or November to early December, at the end of the rains but before Christmas price hikes. September to October tends to be very wet, and floods and mudslides can hamper travel; some regions, like Península de Osa, may close completely.

Left, from top: Isla del Caño reef; Parque Nacional Volcán Poás **Opposite:** Parque Nacional Corcovado

Jasper, Canada

DECEMBER–JANUARY

WHITE-HOT AND SPARKLING

● Is winter the best time to bank the thrills in Jasper? Yep – and the evidence is there in black and white. Up above, the darkest night skies, glittering with constellations; below, snow-gleaming peaks and slopes. Sure, big-name (and big-budget) resorts bag Canadian ski-bucks, but Jasper is powder perfection. And since most outdoors lovers flock here in summer, or head south to Banff in snow season, the pistes are peaceful now.

There are plenty to pick from. On Jasper's doorstep, Marmot Basin features nearly 100 runs across slopes spanning 696 hectares (1720 acres) – and with the highest base elevation of any Canadian ski area, the forecast is great for reliable dumps. Add ample backcountry options and a good mix of green, blue and black runs, and you've a party on the pistes for all abilities.

When the sun goes down, the mountains still beckon – this time for stargazing. Jasper National Park is the world's largest accessible Dark Sky Preserve, with opportunities for stellar astronomical encounters. Visit the planetarium or join an expert-guided telescope experience to roam the cosmos from terra firma – perfect during the long, clear winter nights.

With the town and park rapidly regenerating after the devastating 2024 wildfire, winter stays are more welcome than ever – and every bit as spectacular.

EXPERIENCES

HEAD FOR THE SLOPES: Grab skis or a snowboard to carve some of Marmot Basin's 91 alpine runs; there are also three terrain parks if boxes, rails and jumps are your jam.

REACH FOR THE STARS: Jasper Dark Sky Preserve is one of Canada's largest, with celestial stargazing throughout the long winter nights.

MAKE A BEELINE FOR BACKCOUNTRY: Downhill's not the only game in town: join a guided ski-touring or snowshoe excursion to discover the pleasures of powder.

CONQUER A CASCADE: Frozen waterfalls create spectacular climbing walls; experienced guides make ice-climbing accessible.

NEED TO KNOW

Spending several days on the slopes? Save up to 50% on lift tickets with the Marmot Escape Card, which also bags hefty discounts on accommodation in Jasper. Bring your warmest gear: January's the iciest month, with temperatures rarely nudging above -8°C (17°F), and often dipping much lower. Drivers, don't forget snow tyres or chains – mandatory throughout winter on Icefields Parkway and Marmot Rd.

Left, from top: Marmot Basin; Maligne Canyon, Jasper National Park **Opposite:** Maligne Lake, Jasper National Park

NOVEMBER–FEBRUARY

LOW IS WHEN TO GO

South Carolina, USA

● At first look, winter feels all wrong for the Palmetto State. Its very nickname, coined for the tropical-looking state tree, conjures images of warmth and sunshine. But think again. For a start, it isn't even that cold down by the Atlantic. January highs average 15°C (59°F) – not hot enough for beach-lazing, perhaps, but lovely for coastal strolls and exploring sites and cities. This time also avoids the extremes. Spring is peak tornado season (and besieged by Spring Break crowds). Autumn is worst for hurricanes. Summer seethes with heat and humidity. But winter, it ticks along – cooler, yes, but less oppressive, less expensive, less crowded.

It's good timing for a road trip along the state's 4628km (2876-mile) island-speckled shoreline, mixing natural and cultural attractions. From November to the end of February it's possible to horseback-ride through the surf of touristy Myrtle Beach (it's too busy at any other time of year), and if cold-water swimming is your thing, the waves are a revivifying 10°C (50°F). The historic district and barbecue joints of charming Charleston will be crowd-free. So will the golf courses – plus green rates are lowered for the season. And the birds don't mind the cold, with winter attracting flocks of migratory species.

EXPERIENCES

BIRDWATCH: Winter is peak season at Huntington Beach State Park – highlights include a wealth of waterfowl plus breeding bald eagles.

BAG A BEACH: Take bracing seaside strolls on the trails of rustic Edisto Beach State Park, or go sandboarding on the Outer Banks.

SEE THE CITY: Explore Charleston, from its colourful French Quarter to the buzzing restaurant scene, and visit the sobering Old Slave Mart Museum.

GET TO KNOW THE GULLAH: The Penn Center on St Helena Island deep-dives into the history of the area's Gullah community, established by once-enslaved Africans.

NEED TO KNOW

South Carolina's winters are mild by the ocean but it can drop close to freezing inland, with potential snow on higher ground. For a more typical January break, head to one of the state's ski resorts: Appalachian, Beech Mountain, Cataloochee, Hatley Pointe, Sapphire Valley and Sugar Mountain. Nonskiers could try snowtubing, ice-skating, ice-climbing or hikes out to frozen waterfalls.

Left, from top: Southern-style barbecue dish; Myrtle Beach **Opposite:** Charleston

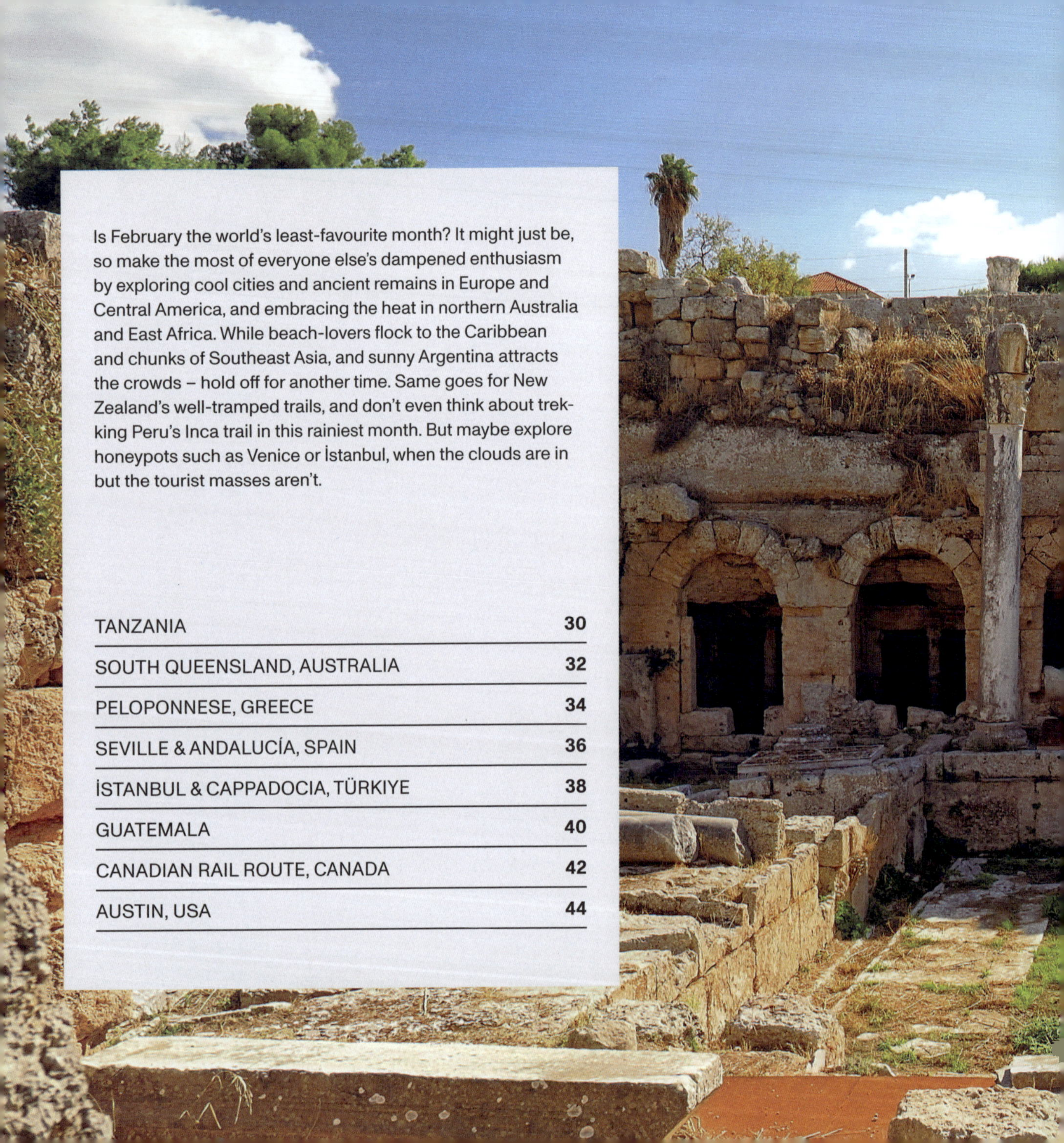

Is February the world's least-favourite month? It might just be, so make the most of everyone else's dampened enthusiasm by exploring cool cities and ancient remains in Europe and Central America, and embracing the heat in northern Australia and East Africa. While beach-lovers flock to the Caribbean and chunks of Southeast Asia, and sunny Argentina attracts the crowds – hold off for another time. Same goes for New Zealand's well-tramped trails, and don't even think about trekking Peru's Inca trail in this rainiest month. But maybe explore honeypots such as Venice or İstanbul, when the clouds are in but the tourist masses aren't.

FEBRUARY

Tanzania

DECEMBER–FEBRUARY

CIRCLE OF LIFE

● The northern Serengeti grabs the (gnus) headlines in July and August, when around 1.5 million wildebeest – plus zebras and prowling predators – brave risky river crossings. But the story starts way down south around February, when hundreds of thousands of wildebeest calve en masse in the southern Serengeti's short-grass plains – a safari spectacle like no other.

As a bonus, visitor numbers drop somewhat in much of Tanzania from around November, bringing prices down and lodge availability up. Sure, you'll likely feel the heat and humidity, but February typically brings a 'short dry' season, improving conditions for wildlife-watching in lush national parks where countless migratory birds arrive and thrive. It's also a fine month to tackle Africa's ultimate trekking challenge: 5895m (19,341ft) Kilimanjaro, the continent's tallest peak and the world's highest freestanding mountain.

And the Serengeti is far from the only safari game in town. Head to the vast Ruaha and Nyerere National Parks – both beautiful and buzzing with wildlife but far less touristed than the Serengeti or Ngorongoro Crater. Among the ribboned river systems of Nyerere, formerly part of sprawling Selous Game Reserve, you've a decent shot at seeing elusive African wild dogs, while Ruaha's rolling hills and plains host most big species – but hardly any other safari-goers.

Left: Trekkers camp, Mt Kilimanjaro **Opposite:** Giraffes, Serengeti National Park

EXPERIENCES

MARVEL AT NEW LIFE: Savour the spectacle of some half-million wildebeest calving in February on the southern Serengeti plains, accompanied by hungry predators.

SNORKEL WITH GIANTS: The planet's largest fish (growing to 10m/33ft and longer), whale sharks cruise off Mafia Island between November and March.

GET AHEAD OF THE GAME: Head to vast, more off-the-radar reserves: Mahale Mountains to track chimps, or Ruaha to watch lions, leopards and even African wild dogs in peace.

CLIMB AFRICA'S ROOF: February's a warm, reasonably dry and quiet time to conquer the trek up mighty Kilimanjaro.

NEED TO KNOW

Tanzania's 'green season' is generally considered to run from November to March, though there's a 'short dry' season from January to mid-March – hot (climbing above 30°C/86°F) and humid, with less rainfall than earlier months. Bear in mind, though, that weather patterns, along with wildlife movements, are becoming less predictable as climate change bites.

FEBRUARY–MARCH

TROPIC THUNDER

South Queensland, Australia

● It's hot. It's wet. It's sticky. But hey, you're in the tropics – what'd you expect? Late summer in Queensland is all of these things – but unlike in the far north here, where the 'Wet' brings serious downpours that put a dampener on most activities, it's much less of an issue in the state's southern half. Sure, some days you can expect to swelter in 90% humidity and 30°C-plus (86°F) heat – but there are some big bonuses. For starters, the sea's reliably 25°C (77°F) and up, perfect for fooling around in the waves. With schools back after the January break, booking accommodation and activities is a breeze, and likely cheaper, too. And epic thunderstorms provide spectacular shows, as well as cooling the air.

Depending on your jam, you'll love the nightlife and wave action on the Gold Coast, south of lively state capital Brisbane, or the mostly mellower vibe on the Sunshine Coast to the north. K'gari (Fraser Island) is uncrowded this month, its crystal-clear creeks and pools limpid and luscious. And the wild hinterland beckons walkers and wildlife-lovers – cool off under a waterfall after tramping the trails through the subtropical rainforest of Lamington National Park, scoping for vivid crimson rosellas, king parrots, pythons and pademelons en route.

EXPERIENCES

SOAK ON THE SANDS: With some 7000km (4350 miles) of coastline, you're never far from a beautiful beach in Queensland, with some of the best in the south.

HEAD FOR THE HINTERLANDS: National parks like Lamington make for epic bush-walking through cloud- and rainforest, keeping eyes peeled for lyrebirds, bower-birds and quolls.

RIDE THE WAVES: Head for the breaks, checking the wind (and local intel) for the best spots, depending on conditions.

GET ARTSY: Brisbane is home to an array of galleries and museums to while away rainy days, plus plenty of edgy street art.

NEED TO KNOW

If your skin's not itching from 90% humidity, the seas off Queensland have another summertime sting in the tail: jellyfish. Though the worst stingers tend to stick to the northern part of the state, it's wise to wear a rash vest. Cyclones that blow up around this time are typically more prevalent further north, too, but again be aware and heed warnings.

Left, from top: Crimson rosella; Lamington National Park **Opposite:** Coolangatta, Gold Coast

Peloponnese, Greece

NOVEMBER–FEBRUARY

EMPTY ANCIENT SITES

● This mountainous, fabulous, fingerlike peninsula, dangling off the bottom of mainland Greece, is relatively quiet year-round – the mass tourism that can mar the country's islands doesn't really exist here. But in winter? The Peloponnese is virtually tourist-free and fairly mild (February highs are 10°–15°C/50°–59°F), so you can wander its storied corners with neither crowds nor withering temperatures.

And there are a lot of storied corners: the Peloponnese is literally legendary. It's where Hercules reputedly performed most of his 12 labours and where Paris eloped with Helen, sparking the Trojan War. It's also where you'll find sites such as Ancient Olympia, where the Olympic Games were held for over 1100 years; Ancient Corinth, home to Jason of Argonauts fame; and Ancient Mycenae, the regal hilltop stronghold of Agamemnon. Indeed, every lofty summit, dense forest, gushing river and precipitous gorge seems to hold some significance.

At this time of year, the upper reaches might even be dusted with snow, opening up unconventional skiing options (try the Ostrakina-Mainalon resort). The snow also adds an extra touch of magic, especially in the central Arcadia region, home to a scattering of traditional villages, historic monasteries, stone-built tavernas and hiking trails.

EXPERIENCES

SEE ANCIENT SITES: So many to choose from: perhaps Nemea, stage for the biennial games held in honour of Zeus; or the Ancient Theatre of Epidaurus.

PERUSE THE PRODUCE: The fertile peninsula excels at producing wines, vegetables, seafood and olives – from November to January, buy cheap raw olives and try preserving them yourself.

STAY BY THE SEA: The Venetian city of Nafplio, crammed with craft shops and topped by a fortress, makes a good base, and remains lively over winter.

HIT THE TRAILS: Most routes are open year-round, including the scenic 75km (47-mile) Menalon Trail.

NEED TO KNOW

The Peloponnese is a 1½-hour drive from Athens. Buses from Athens' main Kifissou Station serve towns such as Nafplio, Kalamata, Sparta and Patras. Trains are slow but scenic. Two lines link Corinth and Kalamata, one across the middle of the peninsula, the other along the north and west coasts. Opening hours of archaeological sites are shorter in winter – many close around 3.30pm.

Left, from top: Raw Peloponnese olives; Nafplio **Opposite:** Ancient Olympia

Seville & Andalucía, Spain

FEBRUARY–MARCH

EUROPE'S WARMEST WINTER

● Winter? What winter? Seville notches up average highs of 18°C (64°F) even in February, over 20°C (68°F) in March. While most of the rest of Europe shivers, Sevillanos are donning light sweaters to spend evenings eating tapas and drinking sherry outside. Rain is a little more common, but in general the weather is rather pleasant – perfect for seeing Seville's grand and varied sites sweat-free, for less, without masses of other people. And mild climes mean nothing stops: you can still ride a horse-drawn carriage around Parque de María Luisa, take a cruise on the Guadalquivir River, or watch a world-class flamenco show – indeed, all rather romantic options if this is a Valentine's trip.

But it's not only Seville. Spring comes early across Andalucía, bringing a sense of awakening. Birds are atwitter and olive picking is underway. White-pink almond blossom fluffs the Sierra Nevada foothills from mid-January; come late February, fragrant orange trees are in bloom. It's a wonderful time for walks between the white villages of the Alpujarras; or even a visit to Parque Nacional de Doñana to witness overwintering birds, as well as the first avian arrivals back from Africa, such as Egyptian vultures, black kites and booted eagles.

Left: Capileira, Alpujarras **Opposite:** Flamenco, Seville

EXPERIENCES

SEE SEVILLE: Queues will be short at the magnificently Moorish Real Alcázar and the grand Gothic cathedral.

PEEK AT THE PUEBLOS BLANCOS: Andalucía's white villages are a delight in winter, when their narrow streets are tourist-free: head to Ronda, Arcos de la Frontera or Grazalema.

EAT LOCAL: Seasonal dishes include *cocido Andaluz*, mixed-meat stew slowly simmered with chickpeas, potatoes, vegetables, herbs and spices; or *puchero*, a wonderfully warming soup – each town has its own recipe.

HIKE THE HILLS: Hit the Alpujarras, to walk amid scenic foothills with the snowcapped Sierra looming above.

NEED TO KNOW

Walking is the best way to explore Seville. Roam between the Barrio de Santa Cruz (Seville's medieval Jewish quarter); riverside El Arenal; El Centro's mazy streets and squares; cool Alameda de Hércules; and characterful Triana, home of flamenco and ceramic tiles. Andalucía's other historic cities can easily be reached by train from Seville: Granada in 2½ hours, Córdoba in 40 minutes.

İstanbul & Cappadocia, Türkiye

DECEMBER–FEBRUARY

WINTER WONDERS

● What's in a name? In Türkiye's largest, most mesmerising city, everything: you can track successive historical eras through its changing monikers, like dating a tree through its rings – from ancient Greek Byzantium through Roman Constantinople and the Ottoman era to buzzing 21st-century İstanbul. Time travel gets 1000% more personal in the depths of winter, when tourists are like hen's teeth and the modern world ebbs away – so you can put yourself in the historical picture at subterranean Roman Basilica Cistern, the astonishing 6th-century basilica-mosque of Hagia Sophia (Aya Sofya), the Ottoman Topkapı Palace and azure-tiled Blue Mosque, plus the labyrinthine Grand and Spice Bazaars and steaming hammams (traditional Turkish baths).

As monuments and hotels empty of visitors, so prices fall: win-win. Thankfully, İstanbul's kitchens serve strong Turkish coffee and warming plates of local delicacies like luscious *İmam bayıldı* (stuffed aubergines) – better yet, learn to make this yourself at a cooking class with a local chef.

Far to the east, yet a short flight away, Cappadocia's fairy chimneys scrape the crisp winter sky: needle-sharp outcrops of volcanic tuff sculpted by aeons of weather and pocked with carved churches and citadels. Enchanting at any time, the region goes full *Game of Thrones* epic under snow.

EXPERIENCES

TRAVEL THROUGH TIME: Roam İstanbul's incredible ancient sites, from underground Roman cisterns and mosaics to Byzantine churches and Ottoman mosques, palaces and hammams.

TAKE TO THE SKIES: Soar through clear winter skies above Cappadocia's fairy chimneys and isolated valleys in a hot-air balloon.

SPICE UP YOUR LIFE: Browse the countless aromatic stalls of İstanbul's Spice Bazaar, then learn to use the delicious bounty at a cookery class.

HEAD UNDERGROUND: Explore Cappadocia's subterranean cities, Derinkuyu and Kaymaklı, used as sanctuaries from various attacking forces for well over a millennium.

NEED TO KNOW

To explore İstanbul on foot with ease, base yourself in the Sultanahmet district on the west bank of the Bosphorus, close to the bazaars, Hagia Sophia, Blue Mosque and most other historic gems. Several flights daily link İstanbul with Cappadocia's airport at Nevşehir in about an hour and 20 minutes. Alternatively, direct buses cover the journey to Göreme in 12 or 13 hours.

Left, from top: Cappadocia; Turkish coffee **Opposite:** Blue Mosque and Hagia Sophia (Aya Sofya), İstanbul

Guatemala

FEBRUARY

GOOD WINTER WINDOW

● Guatemala is a great package, combining active volcanoes, steely blue lakes, rampant jungle, lively markets and a living culture that goes back millennia – some of the finest Maya sites and encounters are found here. In February, it also offers a great window of travel opportunity, when you might just bag the best of all worlds.

In some ways this month is peak season: the weather is pleasantly cool and relatively dry, with highs around 28°C/82°F (though it's chillier and damper in the highlands). But it's also a lull of sorts, straddling the busy December to January holiday period and the spikes of Holy Week, Easter and Spring Break. In short, in-between-y February offers the best climate for exploring, with reduced prices and crowds.

It's also quite easy to get off the tourist trail here. A classic adventure might include the Spanish-era streets of Antigua, dazzling Lake Atitlán, the colourful market in Chichicastenango, a climb up active Volcán de Pacaya or the monumental Maya temples of Tikal. But, equally, you could go further offbeat, hiking to the mysterious forest-swallowed ruins of El Mirador (only reachable on foot), or delving into the remote hills of the Ixil region to experience unique Maya culture.

EXPERIENCES

LEARN THE LINGO: With many language schools, Antigua is an ideal place to brush up on your Spanish.

SEE MORE MAYA: Other fascinating ancient sites include the well-restored trio of Yaxhá, Nakum and El Naranjo; Iximché (close to Antigua); and Copán, over the border in Belize.

ADVENTURE EAST: Cruise the jungly Río Dulce, through its namesake gorge, to arrive on the Caribbean coast at Lívingston, heartland of Guatemala's Garifuna culture.

RIDE A CHICKEN BUS: These bright-painted old North American school buses are a cheap and fascinating way to travel.

NEED TO KNOW

February sees the coffee harvest in full swing. Visit a traditional plantation – found around Antigua and Atitlán – to learn the art of arabica and taste the country's rich, chocolatey brew. The Coffee Harvest Celebration, held early February in Fraijanes, near Guatemala City, is a big shindig, with parades, music and a celebration of the Virgen de la Candelaria (the Black Madonna).

Left, from top: Tikal; Antigua and Volcán de Agua **Opposite:** Chichicastenango Market

Canadian Rail Route, Canada

JANUARY–MARCH

WINTER WONDERS BY TRAIN

● The Rocky Mountaineer is a lightweight – the famed tourist train takes winter off, running only April to October. Not so VIA Rail's mighty Canadian. This 4466km (2775-mile), four-day, four-time-zone-crossing service linking Toronto and Vancouver runs year-round, offering a widescreen look at the country at its sparkliest.

The journey is a cracker: a gradual unfurling of mountains, prairie and the Canadian Shield, with stops in Jasper, Edmonton, Saskatoon and Winnipeg. It delivers swathes of snow-heavy trees, flashes of icy lakes and the sight of lonely grain silos soaring above frost-rimed fields.

On the downside, days are shorter at this time of year, and the temperature outside sure is brisk (maybe -30°C/-22°F). However, the train itself, kitted out with various classes of cabins and dining cars, remains warm and cosy. Plus, tickets are much cheaper (as are hotels in the cities at either end), and the carriages are far quieter – there's no need to fight for a coveted spot in the glass-domed observation cars. As another bonus, in winter Sleeper Plus passengers have unrestricted access to the signature 1950s Park car at the end of the train – in summer, this is reserved for those in fancy Prestige class only.

Left: Observation-Dome views Opposite: Maple Leafs game, Toronto

EXPERIENCES

WINDOW-GAZE: Sit in the Observation Dome and watch the world go by. Or join an onboard talk, tasting or bingo game.

CHAT TO STRANGERS: Share a table in the restaurant car or chat in the bar over a glass of Okanagan red – you never know who you might meet.

CATCH A GAME: Ice-hockey season runs October–April; try to time your ride to coincide with a Vancouver Canucks or Toronto Maple Leafs match.

GO SKIING: Combine a rail ride with the slopes: make a longer stop in Jasper or head to resorts near Vancouver.

NEED TO KNOW

The Canadian runs twice a week: westbound trains leave Toronto Wednesdays and Sundays; eastbound trains leave Vancouver Mondays and Fridays. Three ticket classes are available: Economy (seat only), Sleeper Plus (berth plus meals) and Prestige (cabin plus meals). Short stops are made at stations en route. The train crosses four time zones – onboard announcements tell you when to put your watch forward/back.

DECEMBER–FEBRUARY

MILD AND DELICIOUS

Austin, USA

● The progressive, creative Texan capital lives by the motto 'Keep Austin Weird' – so it makes sense to visit like a weirdo, in the offseason. Winters aren't even that much of a hardship here: February days can be mild, hitting highs around 20°C (68°F). So it's perfectly warm enough to wander the hip stores of South Congress Ave (aka SoCo), or feast at the city's food trucks – you'll find a world of options, from Cajun jambalaya and brisket tacos to Taiwanese pork buns, Lebanese shawarma kebabs, Venezuelan *arepas* (filled maize-flour flatbreads), Brazilian *picanha grelhada* (grilled steak) and warming *om gai* Thai curry.

Attractions such as the distinguished State Capitol and huge Blanton Museum of Art will be less crowded. And, if evenings get chilly, warm up on a bar crawl along historic Rainey St. Or hit the Dirty Sixth (6th St), Austin's rocking strip of restaurants, bars and live-music joints, where there's a party pretty much every night.

To clear your head after the night before, take a dip in Barton Springs Pool, a capacious, turquoise-blue outdoor swim-spot fed by a natural spring that hovers at about 20°C (68°F) year-round – almost balmy for winter swimming. Even better, entrance to the pool is free from November to mid-March.

EXPERIENCES

LOOP LADY BIRD LAKE: The scenic 16km (10-mile) Ann and Roy Butler Hike-and-Bike Trail and Boardwalk runs around the city's much-loved recreational reservoir.

GO TO A GIG: Austin is known as the 'Live Music Capital of the World'; there are venues everywhere, but the Continental Club is a classic spot that opened on South Congress in 1955.

LEARN ABOUT LATINO CULTURE: Austin's Mexic-Arte Museum is a celebration of the traditional and contemporary art and culture of Mexico and Latin America.

EAT MEAT: Take a 45-minute drive to feast in Lockhart, the 'Barbecue Capital of Texas'.

NEED TO KNOW

February is one of Austin's quieter months, though look out for the Austin Marathon (mid-February), when 20,000 runners, and thousands more spectators, flood the city. The route weaves around the main sites, such as Congress Ave and the University of Texas campus. Note, the 10-day SXSW film, media and music festival, held every March, sees crowds boom and hotel prices skyrocket.

Left, from top: Austin food truck; Blanton Museum of Art **Opposite:** Ann and Roy Butler Hike-and-Bike Trail and Boardwalk

Early spring in the northern hemisphere means different things in different places. Much of Western Europe and the USA is balmy and bright, sometimes with showery interludes – hardly scorching beach weather, but quieter than summer. Japan's festooned in cherry blossom, with soaring visitor numbers to match. Hot, sticky conditions arrive in chunks of Southeast Asia, while much of North Africa is blissfully mild – great for hiking in the Atlas, say, or cruising the Nile. Autumn's approaching in Australia, New Zealand, deep South America and South Africa, all of which could be clever shoulder-season options for outdoors adventurers.

MARCH

Uganda

MARCH

GORILLAS IN THE MIST

● Water drips into your eyes – rain or sweat? Either or both – it's hard to tell. You've slip-slide-stomped up steep inclines through the lush forest of Bwindi Impenetrable National Park for hours, following an expert guide along muddy trails. Your mission (and you not only chose to accept it but booked in advance): track one of the park's two-dozen families of mountain gorillas, critically endangered that number just 1000 worldwide. And when you find those gentle great apes, feeding, resting or playing amid the foliage – well, your eyes swim all over again, this time with tears. Meeting our closest cousins can be an overwhelming experience.

Uganda straddles the equator, so it's warm and wet year-round, but rainier and drier seasons dictate visitor numbers. Most come June to September, when gorilla-trekking permits are booked out far in advance; there's another visitor high in less-wet December to February. In March, before the heaviest downpours, deluges still deter many (look for deals at lodges) and make roads and paths more slippery, but also nurture lush vegetation and make for easier chimp-tracking – another premier primate speciality of Uganda. Birds are particularly spectacular, Murchison Falls thunders, and wildlife does what it always does – just with fewer humans getting in the way of your perfect photo.

Left: Mountain gorillas, Bwindi Impenetrable National Park **Opposite:** Murchison Falls

EXPERIENCES

MEET THE RELATIVES: Trek the humid forests of Bwindi Impenetrable National Park for a spellbinding meeting with one of the habituated families of mountain gorillas.

WITNESS THE CASCADE EFFECT: Explore Murchison Falls National Park, where the Victoria Nile surges towards Lake Albert down that namesake cataract.

GO APE: Track chimps through Kibale Forest National Park, watching how troops interact and spotting some of the dozen other primate species that live here.

WATCH WILDLIFE: Head to Queen Elizabeth National Park to look for the famous tree-climbing lions as well as leopards, elephants, buffalos and hyenas.

NEED TO KNOW

Gorilla-trekking permits (valid for one day) must be booked in advance; at the time of writing, they cost US$800 for nonresident foreign visitors. Uganda Wildlife Authority sometimes offers discounted rates during off-peak months – certainly worth checking – but in any case, obtaining one of the few permits allocated for each habituated gorilla family is much easier during the wetter months.

MARCH

LATE-SEASON SPECIAL

Antarctica

● Unless you're a scientific researcher, you wouldn't travel to Antarctica in the true offseason: the austral winter. The lowest temperature ever recorded on Earth was at Vostok Station in July 1983: -89.2°C (-128.6°F). There's a pretty slim window for visiting the White Continent, with the cruise season running from late October to the end of March. Within that, mid-December to mid-February – when the weather is at its warmest, the days at their longest – is the peak period, with the least availability and the highest prices.

However, there are benefits to waiting until March. The temperature is beginning to drop but it will be easier, and cheaper, to secure your booking; plus with fewer ships around, the whole experience will feel more serene. Photographers love this month too, for its low, atmospheric light.

Late February into March is also the best time for seeing large numbers of whales. By now these majestic leviathans are happy, lazy and playful after a summer of feeding on krill – it's not unusual for them to come close to Zodiacs and kayaks. Keep an eye out for humpbacks, minke and even orcas, as well as fur seals – a more common sighting late-season.

EXPERIENCES

PRAY FOR CALM: The stretch of water between the Argentinian port of Ushuaia and the Antarctic Peninsula is notorious and unpredictable: hope for the 'Drake Lake' rather than the 'Drake Shake'.

PICK UP A PADDLE: There's no more intimate way to experience Antarctica's coastline, icebergs and marine life than by kayak.

SAIL INTO PARADISE: There are no guarantees, but with luck your ship will cruise into spectacular Paradise Bay, where snow peaks and glaciers reflect off the seas.

TAKE THE 'POLAR PLUNGE': A leap into freezing Antarctic waters is the ultimate challenge.

NEED TO KNOW

The weather gets colder and the days shorter as the month progresses, so opt for early March if possible. Alternatively, try Antarctica's other sweet spot, in late October and November, at the very beginning of the cruise season: the snow, yet to thaw, is still pristine and untrampled by other cruise passengers, and the penguins are active, breeding and building nests.

Left, from top: Kayaking Antarctic waters; humpback whale, Antarctic Peninsula **Opposite:** Leopard seal, Cierva Cove

Bhutan

FEBRUARY–MARCH

EARLY SPRING, EMPTIER SITES

● Gross National Happiness: that's famously how Bhutan measures prosperity – and the cusp of spring is a sublime time to tap into all that exuberant joy. Head for the Land of the Thunder Dragon in February or March and you'll hear neither the rumble of storms nor the boots of tourist hordes. Not that Bhutan ever gets really overwhelmed – the carefully implemented visa system keeps visitor masses at bay – but most come in October or November to trek before snow blankets high Himalayan trails, or in April for the most famous *tsechus* (festivals).

The weather in lower-altitude Punakha Valley is bordering on balmy, and rhododendron blossoms are starting to burst open, but you'll have the big-wow spots mostly to yourself. We're talking hulking *dzongs* – incredible medieval monastery-fortresses like bulky riverside Punakha – and otherworldly temples such as the Taktshang Goemba, perched improbably on its cliff-side eyrie. In lofty, lonely Phobjikha Valley, you're just in time to admire the graceful courtship dances and bugling calls of breeding black-necked cranes – one of nature's great romantic spectacles. And if you do start to feel the chill, a steaming bowl of Bhutan's national dish, *ema datshi* – fiery chillies in a cheesy sauce – is guaranteed to warm every last cockle.

EXPERIENCES

TACKLE THE TIGER'S NEST: Hike to Bhutan's most famous and photogenic site, the cliff-clinging Taktshang Goemba, aka 'Tiger's Nest Monastery'.

PLAY KING OF THE CASTLE: Climb to mighty Trongsa Dzong, most epic and dramatically set of the monastery-fortresses guarding Bhutan's towns.

HAVE A HOMESTAY: Experience traditional rural living at a Phobjikha Valley homestay, learning about local lifestyles and admiring elegant black-necked cranes before their springtime migration.

TAKE A BOW: Watch a tournament, or even learn the art of archery with a lesson in Bhutan's national sport.

NEED TO KNOW

Bhutan's many *tsechus* (festivals) are legendarily spectacular – and popular: book well ahead (via an authorised tour operator) to experience the biggest draws, such as those in Paro and Thimphu, to thrill to dizzying dances by monks in ornate costumes. Punakha hosts back-to-back (but less-known) dramatic festivals in March – charge camera batteries and empty memory cards in prep.

Left, from top: Festival dancers, Paro; Taktshang Goemba **Opposite:** Bhutanese archer

MARCH–APRIL

EMPTIER ISLES

Eastern Visayas, Philippines

● There are around 7640 islands to choose from across the Philippines – even in peak season (December–February), you should be able to find an atoll, cay or cove to call your own. But for a quieter time in the popular Eastern Visayas – a hot-spot region encompassing islands such as Boracay, Bacolod, Bohol and Cebu – you might want to opt for the shoulder months of March and April instead. Temperatures are starting to heat up (tipping over 30°C/86°F) but rainfall remains low. And crowds are thinner, as long as you work around busy Holy Week, which can affect hotel availability.

Indeed, this is a wonderful time to island-hop, combining flops on palm-swayed white-sand beaches with jungly walks, jeepney rides, ferry trips, dips in crystal-clear springs, wildlife encounters (from warty pigs to hornbills) and explorations of historic Spanish-era towns and traditional villages.

It's brilliant for exploring underwater too – the drier, typhoon-untroubled weather makes for calmer seas and clearer skies, perfect conditions for snorkelling and scuba diving. Head to Moalboal, on western Cebu, to float with huge shoals of sardines; Malapascua Island to swim with thresher sharks; and to the marine reserve of Apo Island for its exquisite coral, gliding turtles and bounty of tropical fish.

EXPERIENCES

MEET MINUTE PRIMATES: Teeny tarsiers, indigenous to the Philippines, are rare these days but may be seen at the sanctuary at Corella, on Bohol.

ADMIRE THE CHOCOLATE HILLS: Bohol's curious cone-shaped mounds – more than 1600 of them – are a designated National Geological Monument.

BE SPELLBOUND ON SIQUIJOR: This dreamy tropical isle has a reputation as a centre of magic and witchcraft; pay a visit to a *mananambal* (traditional folk healer).

BARTER: Spend your pesos at a *tabu*, the colourful weekly village markets where locals gather to sell everything from fresh fish to handicrafts.

NEED TO KNOW

The Philippines' whale-shark season runs November to June, but numbers peak February to April. Swimming with these gentle giants in the wild is popular around Donsol (in the Luzon region, north of the Visayas) and various spots such as Oslob, on Cebu. Outside of Donsol, some whale-shark swims are poorly regulated, with the fish being fed (so altering behaviour); research operators very carefully before booking.

Left, from top: Chocolate Hills, Bohol; green turtle offshore of Apo **Opposite:** Visayas coastline

Alentejo, Portugal

MARCH–APRIL

CHILLED WINE AND WALKS

● Alentejo's ancient history is intoxicating – and not just the Roman remains, megalithic cromlechs and medieval fortifications. Vines were nurtured and harvested in Portugal's largest region long before the Romans arrived 2000 years ago. Today it produces half the country's full-bodied reds and fresh, zingy white wines. Early spring – with wildflowers spangling the hillsides and white storks building twiggy nests on chimneys and clifftops – is the ideal season to plot a grape escape.

With temperatures scooting into the high teens and Alentejo's modest winter rainfall ebbing away, March and April bring balmy days perfect for culinary and cultural discoveries. Come summer, tourists arrive in numbers to roam Évora's walled city, Roman temple and baths, and sunseekers speckle the Atlantic coastline's white-sand beaches. But for now, as chills cede to sunny spring, this already thinly populated region is peaceful, accommodation is easy to find, and restaurants and vineyards are particularly keen to welcome gastronomes and wine-lovers.

Life slows down in Alentejo – literally beyond the Tagus River, stretching east and south of Lisbon towards the Algarve. To ease into the local pace, hike or pedal a stretch of the Rota Vicentina, a network of walking and cycling routes spidering the region's southwestern coast and countryside.

EXPERIENCES

EXPLORE ANCIENT HISTORY: Discover the medieval castles at Évoramonte, Marvão and Mértola; Évora's monumental Sé (cathedral) and Roman remains; Moorish Elvas; and many megalithic monuments.

COAST ALONG THE COAST: Hike or bike the Fishermen's Trail, a 226km-long (140-mile) section of the Rota Vicentina that meanders alongside the dramatic shoreline via white-sand beaches and winsome fishing villages.

GET CRAFTY: Browse local handicrafts in marble towns like Estremoz and Borba.

WINE AND DINE: Trace the Alentejo Wine Route through eight subregions, sampling local drops and traditional dishes such as *açordas* (hearty soups) and *cozidos* (stews).

NEED TO KNOW

Major centres are well served by public transport – Lisbon to Évora is about an hour and 20 minutes by train or bus, Faro to Mértola a little longer. Car hire gives more freedom; bag rentals at Lisbon and Faro Airports. Holy Week isn't celebrated with as much fervour as in neighbouring Spain, but you might encounter ceremonies (and crowds) in some spots at Easter.

Left, from top: Évora dining; Marvão Castelo **Opposite:** Fishermen's Trail at Praia do Malhão

Iceland

MARCH

TRIP THE LIGHT FANTASTIC

● Up for a cosmic science lesson? When solar storms send electrically charged particles surging towards Earth, some zap our planet's magnetic field and, shazam – you get dancing, billowing ribbons and curtains of colour known as aurora.. The weeks around the spring equinox (21–22 March) often bring lively geomagnetic storms, increasing the chances of celestial shows – and though days are stretching out, there's still ample darkness to enjoy the performance on high.

If you're wondering, yup, Iceland's chilly moniker is pretty accurate this month – it's still properly winter, right? So as well as the glaciers that cloak about 11% of the country, right now waterfalls are frozen in photogenic formations, snowshoeing adventures beckon and ice caves are ripe for exploring. True, the mercury doesn't venture much above zero, many campsites close and inland hiking trails are off-limits – but popular sights are peaceful, and accommodation availability better. There are other perks, too: orca are chasing herring off the eerily beautiful Snæfellsnes Peninsula, making for rewarding whale-watching tours.

Reykjavík's never less than sparkling, come snow, rain or shine. Bar and museum-hop your way around this friendliest and perkiest of capitals. And easing back into a hot spring (or geothermally heated tub) at night while northern lights waltz above is little short of magical.

EXPERIENCES

BARHOP IN REYKJAVÍK: Take part in the legendarily epic pub crawl known as the *rúntur*, or just track down the hippest cocktail joints.

HIKE ICE, BABY: Join an ice-cave or glacier-hiking tour in or on the country's biggest ice cap, within Vatnajökull National Park.

WARM UP IN GEOTHERMAL WATERS: Book into big-name Blue Lagoon, or plunge into a public pool or a small natural hot spring (if you're lucky enough to stumble on one).

OGLE ORCA: Board a boat tour in Ólafsvík, on the rugged Snæfellsnes Peninsula, to spot pods of killer whales hunting herring.

NEED TO KNOW

Car hire is the easiest way to get around Iceland. Though backroads in remote areas can be closed by snow in winter (as can the main ring road, Hwy 1), the main routes stay open year-round in the warmer southwest. Iceland is notoriously pricey; book self-catering accommodation where possible to cut down your krónur outlay.

Left, from top: Geothermal hot springs; aurora over central Iceland **Opposite:** Ice-cave hike, Vatnajökull

Naples & Pompeii, Italy

MARCH

MAD WEATHER, EMPTIER SITES

● Admittedly, Italians call this month *marzo pazzo* (mad March) on account of its, er, unpredictable weather. But don't let that put you off an early spring Naples trip. You may or may not get sun or rain, and the 15°C (59°F) highs aren't exactly beachy. But conditions are perfectly fine – if not premium – for exploring the area's wealth of wonderful old stuff at a slower pace, sunstroke-free.

Founded by the Greeks in 470 BCE, Naples' whole historic centre is UNESCO-listed. Amble between its narrow streets, piazzas, palazzi and world-best pizzerias without getting hot and bothered. If the weather does take a nasty turn, delve down into the underground city, a fascinating network of ancient tunnels, aqueducts, caverns and catacombs, 40m (131ft) below.

Mild climes are also perfect for exploring the volcano-buried ruins of Pompeii, to the south. The train to get to the site will be quiet, the crowds inside will be the smallest they'll ever be. And, in cool March, you can keep wandering for hours, to properly take it all in – from Pompeii's brothel to its bathhouse and Anfiteatro, the oldest Roman amphitheatre in existence. Don't miss the House of the Vettii, reopened in 2023 following a 20-year restoration.

Left: Quartieri Spagnoli, Naples Opposite: Neapolitan pizza

EXPERIENCES

SAUNTER SPACCANAPOLI: This narrow, lengthy and animated street dissecting Naples' Centro Storico is the best place to take the city's pulse.

CATCH A PERFORMANCE: Naples' elegant Teatro San Carlo is the world's oldest continuously running opera house; opera season runs November–June.

ROAM RUINS: As well as Pompeii, visit nearby Herculaneum, also buried by the eruption of Vesuvius in 79 CE.

CLIMB VESUVIUS: If you get a clear 'mad March' day, take a trail up the notorious volcano looming over the Bay of Naples – a network of 11 paths weave through Parco Nazionale del Vesuvio.

NEED TO KNOW

Pompeii is 40 minutes from Naples by local Circumvesuviana train. To further minimise the crowds, visit early (the site opens at 9am) on a weekday, which tends to be quieter than weekends. Entrance to Pompeii is free on the first Sunday of the month. Many of Pompeii's finest treasures can be seen back in Naples, at the Museo Archeologico Nazionale.

Patagonia, Argentina & Chile

MARCH–APRIL

AWESOME AUTUMN

● The Americas' far south is the epitome of wilderness: peaks like horns, sparkling lakes, near-endless pampa roamed by wind-blasted llama-like guanacos. Indeed, the sense of scale and mind-bending emptiness is one of Patagonia's biggest draws. So it would be a shame to visit when it's relatively full of other people.

Most travellers come in high summer, December to February, when the weather is at its best (though still fickle) and the prices are ramped up accordingly. But wait until autumn and you're in for a cheaper treat. March and April often experience clear skies and a drop in the ferocity of those Patagonian winds. It's a great time for hiking. The popular trails are much quieter, the *refugios* are easier to book and the landscapes are spectacular: the forests blaze red-gold against the snowcapped mountains and reflect like paintings in the pristine lakes.

Where to go? Maybe drive down from Puerto Montt, in southern Chile, to Villa O'Higgins past lakes and alerce forests, stopping to raft the frothing Futaleufú River (doable into March). Or take the fjord-weaving, four-day Navimag ferry from Puerto Montt to Puerto Natales, trek into craggy Torres del Paine, then hop over to Argentina for fun amid the white tongues of Parque Nacional Los Glaciares.

EXPERIENCES

DO THE 'W': Torres del Paine's classic four-day trek (around 70km/43 miles) links headline sites like Glacier Grey and French Valley. It will be easier to book outside of peak season.

GAWP AT GLACIERS: Pick of the bunch is Perito Moreno, Argentina's 30km-long (19-mile), 5km-wide (3-mile) ice colossus; get closer by boat tour or ice trek.

TACKLE A TREK: The village of El Chaltén is a hiking hub, with a trekking festival staged every March.

GO GAUCHO: Play out those cowboy fantasies at an *estancia* (ranch) amid the Patagonian pampa.

NEED TO KNOW

There are direct flights from Santiago into Chilean Patagonia (to Coyhaique, Punta Arenas, Puerto Natales), and from Buenos Aires into Argentine Patagonia (El Calafate, Esquel, Ushuaia). Patagonian buses are cost-effective and relatively comfortable, with good services during high and shoulder seasons; book tickets well in advance for travel during peak months, and on Fridays and Sundays, which are always busier.

Left, from top: Guanacos, Parque Nacional Patagonia; Glaciar Perito Moreno **Opposite:** Parque Nacional Los Glaciares

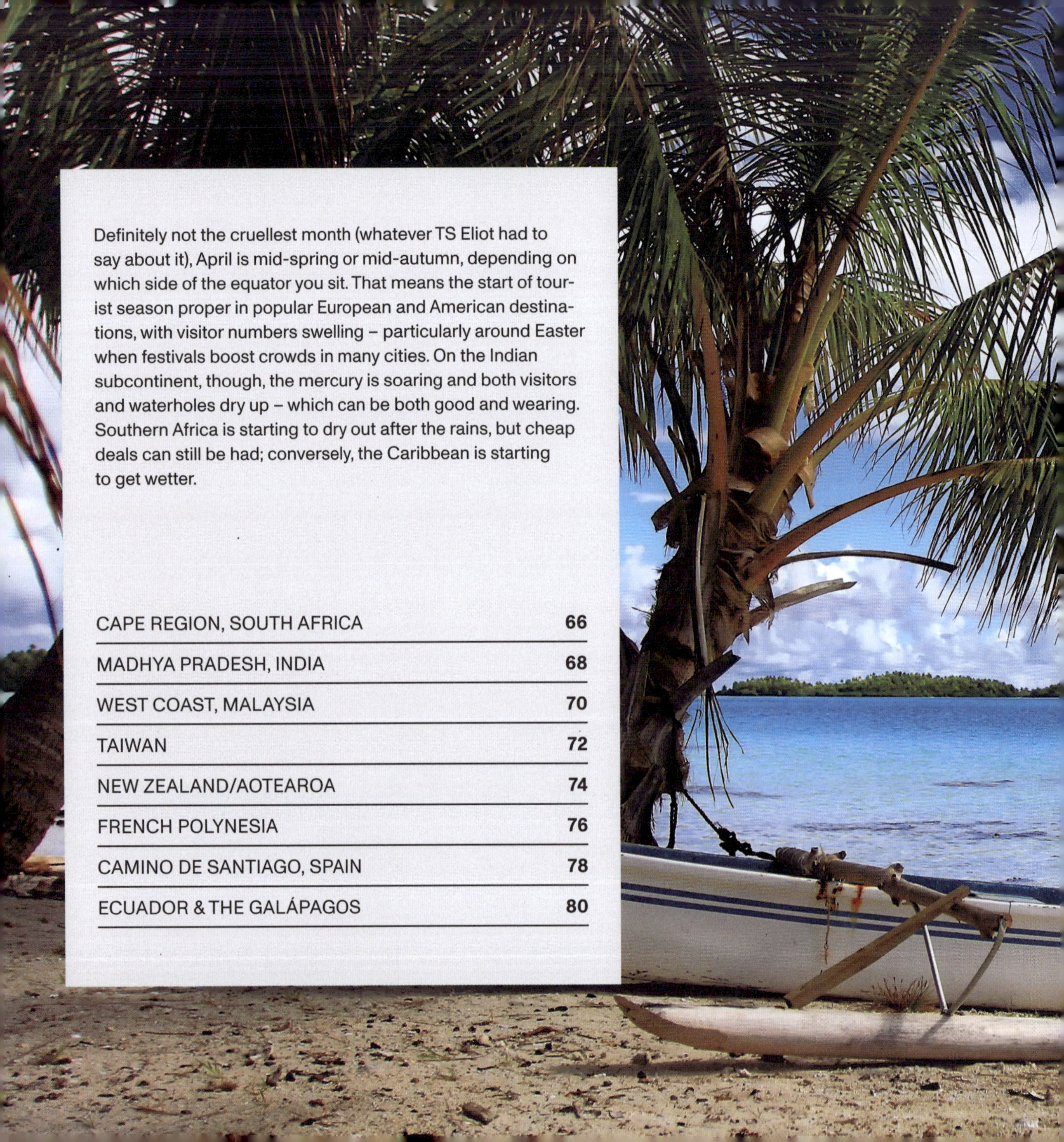

Definitely not the cruellest month (whatever TS Eliot had to say about it), April is mid-spring or mid-autumn, depending on which side of the equator you sit. That means the start of tourist season proper in popular European and American destinations, with visitor numbers swelling – particularly around Easter when festivals boost crowds in many cities. On the Indian subcontinent, though, the mercury is soaring and both visitors and waterholes dry up – which can be both good and wearing. Southern Africa is starting to dry out after the rains, but cheap deals can still be had; conversely, the Caribbean is starting to get wetter.

APRIL

APRIL–MAY

RAINBOW ROAD TRIP

Cape Region, South Africa

● Rainbow forecast: high, and rising. South Africa is dazzling in any season – but as heat eases off and chances of rain start to sneak up across the Cape Region, all that culture, coastal beauty, wildlife and wine come without the visitors who throng here December to March. Accommodation prices subside, too, with good deals in many safari lodges. In fact, this could be the perfect time to steer a self-drive course east through the Rainbow Nation, catching waves and wildlife as you go.

It might be dubbed the 'Mother City', but Cape Town's anything but mumsy. In fact, its other nickname, 'Tavern of the Seas', seems more apt. Work up an appetite tackling Table Mountain, chow down on Cape Malay dishes in colourful Bo-Kaap district, then sip your way round the Wine Route. Veer east to trace the coast on the verdant, forested Garden Route between Mossel Bay and Storms River, maybe pausing for some vitamin sea at Wilderness, Knysna or Plettenberg Bay, or taking to the trails in Tsitsikamma National Park.

You know what you'll find in Addo Elephant National Park – yup, tuskers galore, and great-value safaris – but consider ponying up for solid-gold Big Five wildlife viewing in one of the fabulous private reserves, perhaps Shamwari or Kwandwe.

EXPERIENCES

PLAY CITY SLICKER: Soak up the vibes on Cape Town's V&A Waterfront, choosing from galleries and museums, markets and restaurants as buskers bring the noise.

DRINK IN THE SCENERY: Tour historic estates and taste the finest Shiraz and Cabernet blends at wineries around Stellenbosch and Franschhoek.

TAKE TO THE ROAD: Spend a leisurely few days driving the Garden Route, stopping to chill on beaches and walk in the forests.

WATCH WILDLIFE: Meet mighty pachyderms at Addo Elephant National Park or spring for a more luxe Big Five experience in a private game reserve.

NEED TO KNOW

It's easy (and cheap) enough to hire a car in Cape Town and drive one-way to Chief Dawid Stuurman International Airport at Gqeberha (Port Elizabeth) – allow a couple of weeks to explore Cape Town and wineries, cover the Garden Route at a relaxed pace, and spend a few days on safari. Easter brings an isolated peak in demand – avoid, or book well ahead.

Left, from top: Franschhoek winery; Cape Town's Bo-Kaap district **Opposite:** Shamwari Game Reserve

Madhya Pradesh, India

APRIL–MAY

FIERCE FELINES, FIERCE HEAT

● William Blake's 'tygers' may have burned bright, but in steamy April, it's not just the big cats feeling the heat in much of India. The relatively cool winter becomes a hazy memory this month as temperatures soar, sometimes topping 40°C (104°F) – surely no-one's idea of fun. Except wildlife-watchers. Because in Madhya Pradesh's extraordinary tiger reserves and national parks, vegetation withers and droves of thirsty animals throng streams and waterholes. Ergo, close encounters with the planet's biggest cat – measuring up to 3m (10ft) from nose to striped tail – as well as sambar, spotted and barking deer, langur monkeys, sloth bears, even elusive leopards.

Close to a quarter of India's tigers stalk the region's reserves, and each has its own personality. Pench National Park and Tiger Reserve reputedly inspired Rudyard Kipling's *Jungle Book*; hilly Bandhavgarh has its fort and ample big cats; Kanha's wide meadows offer excellent tiger sightings; compact Panna promises birding and other mammals.

Statewide, you can also snag lower accommodation rates and visit ancient temples and mighty fortresses in peace. Just carry plenty of water and save sightseeing for early morning or late afternoon, avoiding the blast-furnace midday heat.

Left: Gwalior Fort **Opposite:** Tiger, Bandhavgarh National Park

EXPERIENCES

EARN YOUR STRIPES: Take a dawn safari to track tigers in one or more of the famed reserves, also keeping eyes peeled for leopards, sloth bears, monkeys and deer.

BLUSH AT KHAJURAHO'S BEAUTY: Tour two dozen exquisitely decorated Hindu and Jain temples built over a millennium ago, many adorned with erotic carvings.

LEARN ABOUT LOCAL TRIBES: Discover the rich cultural heritage of the region's varied peoples at Bhopal's dizzying Tribal Museum.

STORM A FORTRESS: Roam vast Gwalior Fort, an ancient, elaborate bastion built atop a high plateau and now home to palaces, temples and museums.

NEED TO KNOW

Though tourist numbers in India generally dip from March, wildlife cognoscenti (especially local game-watchers) are keen to experience the best conditions for spotting tigers and other species in April and May, so it's wise to book reserve permits and accommodation well in advance. Hotels elsewhere in the state can get busy at Easter, too. Tiger reserves are typically closed on Wednesdays.

West Coast, Malaysia

MARCH–MAY

SUNSHINE ON YOUR SHOULDER

● Spicy, luscious, varied, tangy, colourful and aromatic, melding a lucky dip of influences from across Asia – Chinese, Indian, Thai, Indonesian and more. We're talking Malaysian food, but could just as well be describing this incredible country. It's a steaming hotpot of cultures, wildlife and experiences, with a climate as mixed as its cuisine. In western parts of the peninsula, including sun-and-sand hot-spots like Langkawi and Penang, the drier months (December to February) draw peak visitor numbers. Make the most of the shoulder season that follows, before the heaviest rains but when you might snag discount room rates.

You could spend a fortnight lounging on Langkawi's white-sand beaches. But you'd be missing out on the blended Peranakan (Chinese-Indian-Malay) culture of Penang; the tea plantations around Cameron Highlands; the wildlife of Taman Negara National Park (spot elephants, monkeys, hornbills and tapirs or, if super-lucky, tigers and rhinos). Then there's capital Kuala Lumpur's buzzing contemporary art scene, blingy Batu Caves and historic Dutch architecture in metro Melaka.

And don't miss that food. Stall-hop Lot 10 Hutong and Petaling St in KL, slurp spicy laksa (noodle soup) at food markets in George Town, Penang, or take a cookery class in Melaka.

EXPERIENCES

MEET MARINE LIFE: Hop from Langkawi's beaches to plunge beneath balmy waves for a spot of snorkelling in Pulau Payar Marine Park.

EXPLORE PENANG: Discover historic merchants' mansions, Chinese temples, tropical spice gardens and charismatic wildlife in Penang National Park.

MAKE A DATE FOR TEATIME: Roam the lush plantations that surround hill stations such as Cameron Highlands, and savour local flavours during a tea tasting.

PERFECT YOUR PERANAKAN: Learn how to cook authentic Nyonya cuisine at a cookery school in Melaka.

NEED TO KNOW

Malaysia's climate can be mind-meltingly confusing: between March and May, when it's drier on the east coast of the peninsula, Kuala Lumpur's getting hammered, Langkawi's wet season is just getting started – and Borneo's another story altogether. This is the tropics, after all; it's perennially hot and humid, so best to assume you'll get some rain wherever and whenever you visit.

Left, from top: George Town street food; Boh Sungei Palas Tea Estate, Cameron Highlands **Opposite:** Dhammikarama Temple, George Town

Taiwan

MARCH–APRIL

SPRING FESTIVAL FEVER

● Taiwan's a firecracker – and that's no secret. When cherry blossoms festoon parks and Chinese New Year sparks celebrations, it gets busy. When winter weather is cool and pleasant, from December – busy. Even during the crazy hot and humid typhoon months of July and August – busy. Conversely, during the drab grey skies and downpours of the 'plum rain season' (May–June), much of Taiwan just isn't where you want to be.

April, though – that's spring perfection. The air's warming up but still fresh (nudging 23°C/74°F in Taipei, even warmer down south around Kaohsiung). The sea's pleasant enough for a dip, but beaches are quiet. Hiking trails beckon in near-perfect conditions, and music festivals sparkle – yet tourists are sparse and there are deals to be had. What's not to love?

City slickers enjoy hefty hits of history and culture – temples, galleries, world-class museums (don't miss Taipei's National Palace Museum) – plus Taiwan's trademark salty-sweet cuisine, influenced by flavours from mainland China, Japan and indigenous dishes. National parks are verdant and alive: if you missed the tail-end of cherry-blossom season, gawp at carpets of blooming calla lilies around Zhuzihu in Yangmingshan National Park. The weather's great for ambling, too, whether hopping between city street-food outlets or along mountain trails.

EXPERIENCES

TASTE TAIWAN: Try Taipei's food stalls, Keelung's Miaokou Night Market, or the traditional snack shops around Anping Fort in Tainan, particularly along Yenping St.

TAKE TO THE TRAILS: Hike between the marble rockfaces of Taroko Gorge, alongside Sun Moon Lake; or up Taiwan's second-tallest peak, Xueshan (Snow Mountain).

ENJOY ISLAND LIFE: Relax on one of the dozens of islands of the Penghu Archipelago, lounging on golden-sand beaches or trying your hand at windsurfing.

SEE TERRIFIC TEMPLES: Visit beautiful and colourful Taipei temples like lovely Longshan or 200-year-old Bao'an.

NEED TO KNOW

Festivals can make for unforgettable experiences – but also crowds and heavily booked accommodation, particularly during Chinese New Year (late January or early February, when many restaurants also close), and the spectacular Lantern Festival a couple of weeks later. There's also a four-day, long-weekend public holiday in early April, which may affect your plans. October's another great month to visit.

Left, from top: Sun Moon Lake; Zhuzihu, Yangmingshan National Park **Opposite:** Taipei night market

MARCH–APRIL

ACTIVE AUTUMN

New Zealand/ Aotearoa

Summer's the sweetest in the other Down Under, right? Well, maybe – but, given NZ's four-seasons-in-one-day rep, mellower, quieter autumn is pretty near perfect, especially if outdoors action is your thing. It's still mostly warm and dry but, being shoulder season, far less busy – so you can book later, keep timings flexible and bag savings on rooms, tours and transport.

The toughest call is choosing from the lengthy menu of active options. Hiking's the nailed-on number-one – but in April, end of the trekking season, fewer people tackle the multiday Great Walk treks. The Milford, Routeburn and Heaphy tracks top most walkers' wish lists, but the other eight (including the Whanganui Journey, a river voyage by canoe) are equally epic. You'll want to pack waterproofs and warm layers in autumn – but the same advice holds in January. And with forests aflame with autumn foliage, this is a spectacular season to tackle these spectacular routes.

Passion for pedalling? Head out on the 2500km (1553 miles) of mountain-bike-friendly routes that link Aotearoa's top and tail. Fjord focus? Take a cruise on Milford Sound/Piopiotahi, lined with waterfall-striped ridges and peaks, or peaceful Doubtful Sound/Patea – and expect to be escorted by an honour guard of bottlenose dolphins. Grape expectations? Autumn is harvest-o-clock, ideal for winery tours.

EXPERIENCES

TAKE A HIKE: Tackle one of the 11 Great Walks – multiday treks traversing New Zealand's most spectacular landscapes – or day-hikes such as the Tongariro or Pouākai Crossings.

PLOT A GRAPE ESCAPE: Tour vineyards in regions such as Marlborough and Queenstown during the harvest.

SADDLE UP: Pedal one of 23 Ngā Haerenga Great Rides of New Zealand along ridges, around fjords and through forests blazing with autumn foliage.

MAKE A SOUND INVESTMENT: Board a cruise to discover the impossibly photogenic, dolphin-cruised fjords cleaving the south-west coast of the South Island.

NEED TO KNOW

To hike one of the 11 Great Walks *(doc.govt.nz/great-walks)* during the official October–April season, when huts are open and most facilities available, you'd best bag a place pretty much as soon as bookings open – usually late May or early June. If you don't snag a spot, consider an alternative trek – the Queen Charlotte Track through the magnificent Marlborough Sounds, say.

Left, from top: Marlborough vineyard; Milford Sound/Piopiotahi **Opposite:** Along the Tongariro Crossing

French Polynesia

APRIL–MAY

CUT-PRICE PARADISE

● Arguably, the 120 or so volcanic and coral isles of French Polynesia – including Tahiti, Bora Bora and the magnificent Marquesas – are your stereotypical paradises all year long. Floating in the South Pacific, a little below the equator, they're perpetually warm, sunny, palm-swayed and exquisite, with temperatures deviating little off 30°C (86°F). But April to May is a good choice if you're looking to cast yourself away without the crowds.

At the tail end of the wetter period (which runs November–April), it's also neatly before the June–August holiday peak. So while a few short, sharp showers might dampen an afternoon, those white-sand beaches will be far less busy, those dreamy stilted villas more competitively priced. April also augurs the beginning of the main diving season, when lighter breezes leave the water calm and clear – all the better for finning about with an array of rays, turtles and sharks.

For a different take on these far-flung isles, book a berth aboard the *Aranui*. This hybrid cruise ship/freighter is responsible for resupplying minuscule, remote communities, providing a lifeline for islanders, and therefore runs year-round. Itineraries vary, but passengers (who sleep in comfortable cabins crammed in among the cargo) enjoy a unique insight into Polynesian life.

Left: Bora Bora Opposite: Snorkelling off Mo'orea

EXPERIENCES

DELIGHT IN A DIVE: The Tuamotu Islands (Rangiroa, Fakarava, Manihi, Tikehau) and knockout Bora Bora are thrilling scuba spots, especially Rangiroa's shark-filled Tiputa Pass.

BE INSPIRED: Artist Paul Gauguin immortalised the islands of French Polynesia; make a pilgrimage to his grave on Hiva Oa, in the wildly remote Marquesas Islands.

MAKE FOR MO'OREA: A 30-minute ferry-hop from Tahiti, this idyllic isle is home to dazzling Cook's Bay and a network of adventurous hiking trails.

SHIMMY INTO CULTURE: The hypnotising Ori Tahiti Festival, held in April, is a vibrant celebration of Polynesian dance.

NEED TO KNOW

Tahiti-Faa'a Airport, near Tahiti's capital Papeete, is an eight-hour flight from LA, five from Auckland, 22 from Paris. Air Tahiti flies to almost 50 islands and atolls across the country. Ferries link Tahiti and Mo'orea, and Tahiti and the other Society Islands. Passenger/cargo vessels sail to the Marquesas and Austral Islands every two weeks, and to the Gambier Islands once a month.

Camino de Santiago, Spain

MARCH–EARLY MAY

PRE-PEAK PILGRIMAGE

● In the Middle Ages, the ultimate holy escapade was a trek to the shrine of St James. Fast forward to today, and guess what? The Camino de Santiago is having a moment again – around 500,000 people lace up their boots each year to hit this iconic network of trails. Pilgrimage: it's officially back in style.

Sure, part of the charm is the buzz of camaraderie with fellow *peregrinos* (pilgrims, if you're new here), but if you're after a deeper, more Zen-like experience, timing is everything. May, June and September are popular months, with warm days, long evenings and lively trails without the full-on summer crush; July and August bring serious heat and hordes of holidaying Spaniards. Winter, on the other hand, is quiet and magical in its own way, though you'll face frosty mornings, snow on the higher ground and fewer cafes and hostels open for business.

April, though? It's the sweet spot. The landscapes are all lush-green and birdsong-y, the weather's just right for walking (hello, top temps of 17°C/63°F), and the trails are pleasantly lively without feeling overwhelmed. This is the perfect month for soaking in the spiritual vibes and box-fresh scenery with like-minded souls.

EXPERIENCES

STAY IN ALBERGUES: The best way to get to know fellow pilgrims is sharing a dorm room with them.

STAND IN PLAZA DEL OBRADOIRO: The grand square before Santiago's cathedral is journey's end – a place of sore knees and soaring spirits.

GET CERTIFIED: To earn a *Compostela* (certificate of completion) you must walk at least the last 100km (62 miles) to Santiago, getting your *credencial* (pilgrim passport) stamped en route.

DINE TOGETHER: From tasty tapas to cheap, three-course Menú de Peregrinos, it's not about what you eat but who you eat with.

NEED TO KNOW

There are multiple 'Ways of St James'. Busiest by far is the Camino Francés (around 770km/478 miles) from St-Jean-Pied-de-Port in France; the final 100km (62 miles) from Sarria to Santiago is the most crowded section. Others include the Camino Portugués from Lisbon (about 620km/385 miles), the Portugués Coastal from Porto (260km/162 miles) and the Camino Inglés from Ferrol (120km/75 miles).

Left, from top: Seafood paella with Peregrina beer in Galicia, Spain; St-Jean-Pied-de-Port, Camino Francés **Opposite:** Camino Primitivo

Ecuador & the Galápagos

APRIL–MAY

WET AND WILD

● South America's pocket-rocket packs a powerful punch of colour. There's the zingy emerald green of the Amazon Rainforest. The greens and reds of marine iguanas, scarlet-balloon-throated frigatebirds, poppy-and-cornflower Sally Lightfoot crabs, pink flamingos and dancing blue-footed boobies in the Galápagos. Emeralds, lilacs and yellows of tanagers, toucans and hummingbirds in the cloud forest.

The northern hemisphere summer and Christmas holidays, which coincide with drier days, bring an influx of tourists. But, get this – the wetter, quieter months win out in most regions.

Take the Galápagos: April and May bring warm, clear, calm days and seas, perfect for snorkel excursions where you might spot playful young sea lions, turtles and penguins. Breeding birds and marine iguanas don courtship colours, and afternoon showers freshen things up.

The rainforest is, of course, rainy – rivers swell and forests flood, so exploring by boat is easiest, getting you up close to monkeys and birds feeding amid the flowering canopy. Highlands, too, can be soggy, but lace up boots to hike beneath the symmetrical cone of Volcán Cotopaxi, or simply explore Quito's Old Town, studded with Spanish-era, neoclassical and baroque churches and palaces.

EXPERIENCES

TAKE A SNORKEL SAFARI: Fin Galápagos waters on the lookout for penguins, inquisitive young sea lions, graceful turtles, and marine iguanas grazing on algae.

BROWSE INDIGENOUS MARKETS: Delve into the rainbow shades of bazaars at Otavalo or Saquisili.

ROAM THE RAINFOREST: Join an expert-led tour to the Amazon region, spotting profuse birdlife, insects and tree frogs.

BE DAZZLED IN QUITO: Amid the glorious churches and mansions you'll find world-class museums and galleries, including the Museo Nacional, packed with pre-Hispanic art including super-bling golden artefacts.

NEED TO KNOW

Though April and May are typically the rainy low season across Ecuador, big festivals – especially Semana Santa (Holy Week) leading up to Easter – see crowds and prices soar and rooms at a premium. Either avoid those dates or, if you're keen to experience these colourful celebrations – especially the spectacular Good Friday procession in Quito – book well in advance.

Left, from top: The Otavalo market in Quito, Ecuador; Snorkelling off Santa Cruz Island, Galápagos **Opposite:** Toucan, Amazon Rainforest

APRIL–MAY

PRE-CROWD CLASSIC COAST

Cape Cod, USA

● If you're fond of sand dunes and salty air, quaint little villages here and there, you're sure to fall in love with old Cape Cod, Massachusetts. Though you might love it less if you go in swarming summer: Cape Cod National Seashore receives around 680,000 visitors in July.

By contrast, January gets around 105,000 – but it can be chilly and closed for business. April, however, is a good middle ground: visitors number around 240,000, temperatures climb to about 12°C (54°F) and, importantly, the optimism of spring is in the air. There's a sense of the place gearing up for the season. Cherry trees are blossoming, and parks and gardens are beginning to bloom – check out Sandwich's Heritage Museums and Gardens. Whale-watching trips start to run at weekends from Provincetown and Hyannis, and the alewife herring are running in Plymouth – this frenzied dash of fish through the town's waterways is celebrated with the Plymouth Herring Festival, on the third Saturday in April.

And while it might not be sunbathing weather, the coast is still great. Go beachcombing, look for birds (Cape Cod is a key spring rest stop for many migratory species), and take wild, windswept walks for a refreshing dose of that salty air.

Left, from top: Lobster roll and fries; Crown & Anchor, Provincetown **Opposite:** Cape Cod shoreline, Provincetown

EXPERIENCES

CHOW DOWN: Cape classics include warming bowls of chowder, fried clams and fresh lobster – just coming into season in April.

TAKE A SPRING RIDE: The 40km (25-mile) Cape Cod Rail Trail is an easy pedal from Yarmouth to Wellfleet via port towns, beaches, salt marshes, pine forests and cranberry bogs.

STROLL THE SHORE: The Cape Cod National Seashore's Salt Pond Visitor Center is open year-round; numerous trails lead from here.

EXPLORE PROVINCETOWN: Big enough to stay lively year-round, Provincetown has plenty of restaurants, galleries, hip boutiques and cosy bars.

NEED TO KNOW

April offers lower rates and higher availability on Cape Cod, though hotels can get busy around Patriots' Day (third Monday of April). Enough businesses are open year-round to make a trip perfectly feasible, especially if you stay in the larger towns. Things get going in earnest from late April. Fast ferries from Boston to Provincetown start running mid-May.

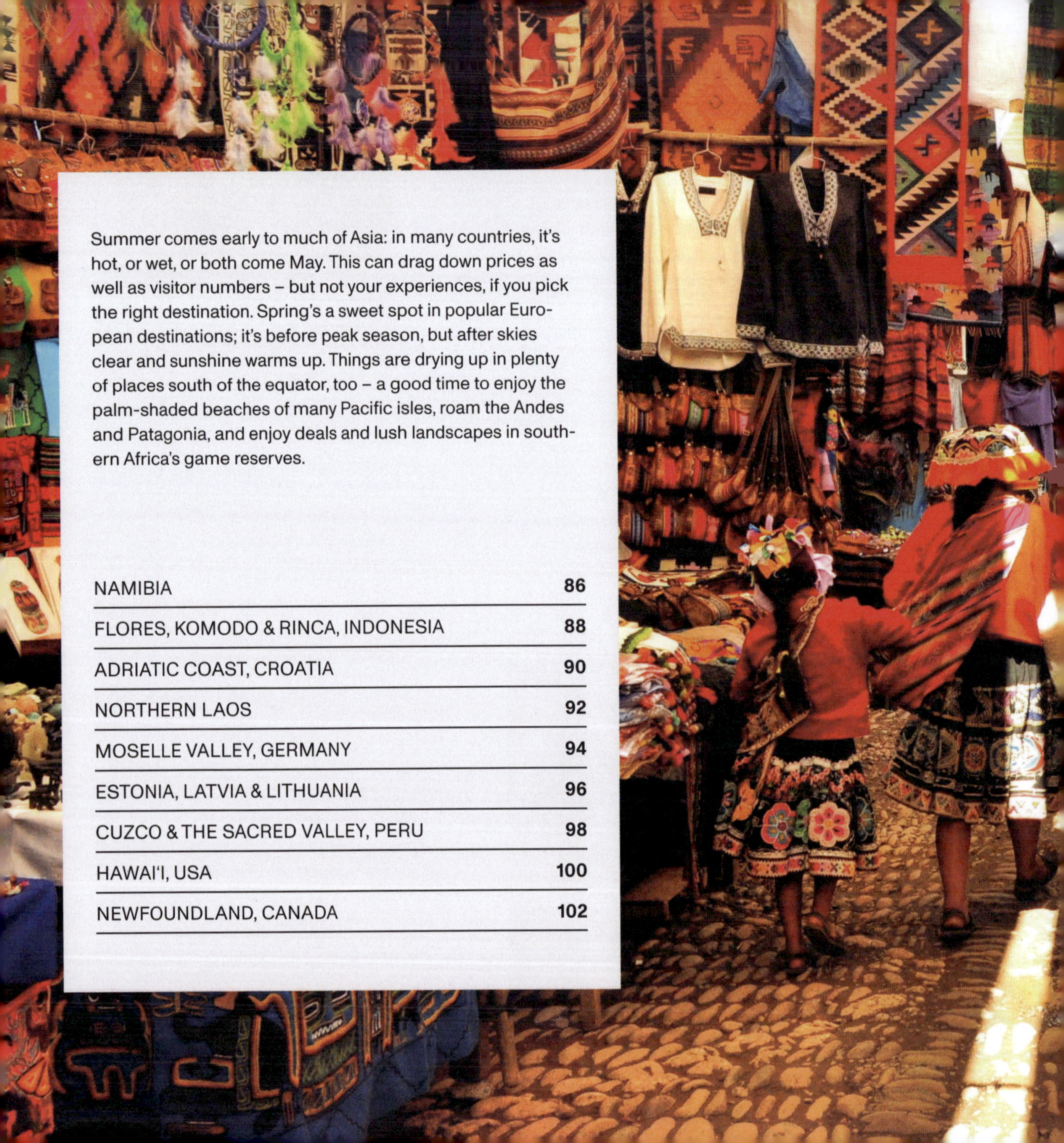

Summer comes early to much of Asia: in many countries, it's hot, or wet, or both come May. This can drag down prices as well as visitor numbers – but not your experiences, if you pick the right destination. Spring's a sweet spot in popular European destinations; it's before peak season, but after skies clear and sunshine warms up. Things are drying up in plenty of places south of the equator, too – a good time to enjoy the palm-shaded beaches of many Pacific isles, roam the Andes and Patagonia, and enjoy deals and lush landscapes in southern Africa's game reserves.

MAY

Namibia

APRIL–MAY

DESERT AT ITS PRIME

● Spring is special in Namibia. It's a chance to see this famously arid, dramatically desert-dominated country at its most lush – but without getting wet. Namibia's rains begin in December and tail off in March; by April, landscapes are gloriously green and the skies are cleansed of dust and crystal clear. It's a great time for photography.

Also photogenic are the animals that, feasting on this natural abundance, are looking fabulously well. True, they can be harder to spot: the thicker foliage is obstructive and they're not forced to congregate at limited water sources. But this adds extra thrill to the chase. And Namibia has some excellent guides on hand to help. Even better, lodge rates are significantly lower in April and May, before peak season starts.

At this time you might see the sinuous dunes of the Sossusvlei region sprinkled with foliage. Or flashes of green against the saltpans of Etosha National Park. The humpbacks won't yet have arrived around Walvis Bay, but pelicans, dolphins and the noisy Cape fur seal colony can be seen year-round. The temperatures are lovely too, with pleasant daytime highs of around 25°C (77°F), dropping to around 13°C (55°F) at night – not too nippy for gazing up at Namibia's stellar dark skies.

EXPERIENCES

SPOT CATS: The AfriCat Foundation's Okonjima Nature Reserve, in Namibia's Central Highlands, offers excellent chances of glimpsing leopard and cheetah.

UP THE ADRENALIN: The German-built coast town of Swakopmund is a hub for white-knuckle activities, from dune-boarding to sky diving.

ENTER THE NAMIB: At 50,000 sq km (19,305 sq miles), Namib-Naukluft National Park is one of the biggest in the world; opt for hot-air balloon flights, stargazing nights, canyon scrambles and nature walks.

ENCOUNTER EVERYTHING: Namibia's flagship park, Etosha is teeming with life, from giraffes and elephants to endangered black rhinos.

NEED TO KNOW

Self-drive is a straightforward option here: distances are vast but the region has good roads (some tarmac, some gravel). A 4WD isn't required unless you plan to travel well off-grid. Traffic is exceptionally light, even in peak season. Be sure to carry plenty of supplies, as if you're unlucky enough to break down, it may be a while before help arrives.

Left, from top: Cape fur seal, Swakopmund; leopard in Okonjima Nature Reserve **Opposite:** Etosha National Park

Flores, Komodo & Rinca, Indonesia

APRIL–JUNE

WILD ISLANDS

● Here be dragons! Or at least the nearest thing surviving today: Komodo dragons, giant monitor lizards known locally as *ora*. Growing over 3m (10ft) long and weighing 70kg (154lb) and up, these fearsome creatures tackle prey as large as water buffaloes via a bite laced with venom and bacteria. In short, they're not to be messed with.

They are, though, quite the spectacle. And the transition months following the end of the heaviest rains, when the waters are calm but before the peak July–August tourist season, are ideal for tracking these incredible predators – in the company of an experienced local guide, of course. Found only in Komodo Island's namesake national park and on neighbouring Rinca, Padar and Flores, *ora* are now gearing up for mating season, when dramatic fights break out between rival males.

The endangered reptiles aren't the only attractions, though. In the national park you can spot deer, monkeys, boar and a host of birdlife; beneath the waves, reef fish flit among the coral, joined by turtles and rays. There's more colour in the highlands of Flores: hike to the multihued crater lakes of Gunung Kelimutu and smaller Wawo Muda, and visit Manggarai and Ngada communities maintaining traditional customs amid breathtaking volcanic landscapes.

EXPERIENCES

MEET THE MONITORS: Join a local guide to seek out dragons on Komodo or Rinca.

SAIL THE SEAS: Board a *phinisi* (sailing ship) for the three- or four-day voyage from Lombok to Labuan Bajo, stopping at Komodo, and snorkelling (perhaps seeing whale sharks) at Saleh Bay.

CLIMB FLORES' CRATERS: Take a sunrise trek to the lake trio atop Kelimutu, their various colours changing over time.

SNORKEL THE REEFS: Discover dazzling marine life in the waters off Komodo – fin out from Pantai Merah (Pink Beach) or around Pulau Lasa.

NEED TO KNOW

You can fly direct to Labuan Bajo, the port town in western Flores that's the jumping-off point for Komodo and Rinca, from Denpasar (Bali), Jakarta or Kuala Lumpur. Entrance fees apply for Komodo National Park, including Rinca Island – 250,000 rupiah (about US$15) for foreign tourists at the time of writing, plus additional costs levied for guides, snorkelling, hiking and other elements.

Left, from top: Komodo Island ora; Kelimutu Crater, Flores **Opposite:** Wae Rebo Village, Flores

Adriatic Coast, Croatia

MAY

SHORE THING

● Stardom can be hard to handle – even for old-timers like Dubrovnik. Sure, Croatia's most famous city enjoyed celebrity before in its medieval heyday, yet the terracotta-roofed walled Old Town wasn't prepared for the mass attention *Game of Thrones* inspired. And with cheap flights and cruise ships disgorging thousands of visitors daily, the city groans in July and August.

May, though – this is when sun and serenity combine on Croatia's coast. As daytime temperatures climb to around 23°C/74°F (and seas warm almost as fast), hotels and restaurants fling open windows, and ferries resume normal service after the winter break. Not only do far fewer tourists throng the marble streets that body-doubled for King's Landing – other hot-spots that attract the crowds in high summer also chill in balmy May. Take Split, where you can wander the incredible palace complex (built by Roman emperor Diocletian as his retirement home) without being jostled. Or the dozens of idyllic islands speckling the Adriatic: the clubbers are yet to flock to Hvar's Venetian-era Old Town; the beaches of Brač, Pag and Lopud are still spacious and calm; warm days are perfect for savouring the crisp white Grk, Pošip and Rukatac wines of Korčula.

Left: Old Town and harbour, Hvar **Opposite:** Zlatni Rat, Brač

EXPERIENCES

SET SAIL: Board a small ship to cruise calm, balmy seas and explore southern Adriatic islands such as Hvar, Mljet and Korčula in peaceful spring.

DRINK TO YOUR HEALTH: Explore lovely Lošinj, renowned as the 'Island of Vitality' for its pellucid waters and clean air scented with pine and medicinal herbs.

CELEBRATE A SAINT: Experience processions, music and street fairs as Split commemorates its patron saint, Domnius, on 7 May.

FEAST ON FINE CUISINE: Tuck into local specialities like Istrian asparagus or seafood risotto in Dalmatia, washed down with a white Malvazija wine.

NEED TO KNOW

Autumn (especially late September into October) is another great time to visit Croatia: the crowds have receded and prices have dropped, but the Adriatic is still warm enough for swimming. Figs and pomegranates are ripe, and Istria's truffle season is in full swing. From November to April, many coastal and island hotels and restaurants close and ferry services are reduced; costs also fall, though.

Northern Laos

MAY

TRIBES AND TEMPLES

● Mountains and the Mekong, hill-tribe villages and ancient temples, delicious food and legacies of Indochinese wars – no, not Vietnam. Little sibling Laos has all these attractions but a fraction of the visitors, especially after the rainy season begins to bite. Most travellers opt for the dry months of November to April; while May gets superhot and showers start in earnest, the downpours are usually brief evening affairs that leave the air fresher – and mean sparser crowds. The further south you go, the wetter it'll get – head north for the best weather.

The chunk of country above capital Vientiane crackles with cultural and natural wonders. Perched where the Khan and Mekong Rivers meet, Luang Prabang is an alluring little town packed with gorgeous gilded temples and French-Indochinese villas, and it's unsurprisingly popular. Keep on keeping on for more secrets and surprises. You might stumble over giant megalithic vessels scattered across the Plain of Jars; roam the lush forested hills and waterways of Nam Et-Phou Louey National Park or Nam Ha Protected Area for intimate wildlife encounters; or hike between hill-tribe hamlets near Luang Namtha. Don't be alarmed by sudden bangs: the Bun Bang Fai (Rocket Festival) explodes into life around this time.

EXPERIENCES

MAKE FOR THE HILLS: Trek between remote Ikhor and Hmong villages in the highlands around Luang Namtha.

MEET THE MONKS: Join those giving alms to the saffron-robed Buddhist monks of Luang Prabang's glittering gilt-roofed temples.

GO UNDERGROUND: Explore the extensive Vieng Xai Caves, riddling dramatic limestone karst scenery, to see where thousands sheltered from conflict in the 1960s and early 1970s.

RELAX BY THE RIVER: Chill in the sleepy riverside village of Nong Khiaw, alongside the Nam Ou, tucking into *laap* (pork salad), spicy shredded green papaya and other traditional Lao dishes.

NEED TO KNOW

At the end of the March–April dry season, the mercury ratchets up and many farmers burn fields, creating a choking haze. May can be steamier still – 30°C (86°F) and up – with increasing rainfall, but travel is mostly more enjoyable, though journeys can take longer in remote areas with dirt roads. A single-entry e-visa is valid for 30 days; apply at least five days in advance.

Left, from top: Wat Mai, Luang Prabang; Lao-style *khao poon nam prik* (noodle soup) **Opposite:** Nam Ou river, Nong Khiaw

Moselle Valley, Germany

MAY

CYCLING, CASTLES, CHEERS

● Forecast for the Moselle in May: sunny and warm, with occasional drops of Müller-Thurgau and Riesling. This mesmerising, meandering valley's sheer sides are striped with vines and studded with *Weinguts* (wineries) that fling open doors for tastings as spring days lengthen. And while we don't encourage drinking and biking, you can easily hop off your steed for modest tastings and stock up for sipping later, after bikes are back in racks.

May and the Moselle are made for each other. With long days, temperatures tickling 20°C (68°F), a host of wine festivals and the restart of ferry services – but before families and oenophiles arrive to pack picture-perfect medieval towns and wine terraces – this month is pedalling perfection. Linking vineyards and forts, the 248km (154-mile) Moselle Cycle Path traces the river's curves between Perl on the Germany–France–Luxembourg border and the confluence with the Rhine at Koblenz. It's a flat and mostly off-road trail, with ample high-calibre campsites, hotels and wineries en route.

And then there's the castles. Like the Rhine's (but far less touristed), the Moselle's meanders are guarded by bastions in various states of romantic ruin, from Traben-Trarbach's eerie Starkenburg and Grevenburg to Cochem's whimsically reconstructed Reichsburg. All in all, a bibulous biking treat.

EXPERIENCES

ROAM ROMAN REMAINS: Explore the ancient basilica, baths, amphitheatre and Porta Nigra (Black Gate) in Trier, considered Germany's oldest city.

CLIMB TO CASTLES: Visit the various spectacularly set fortresses – don't miss romantically ruined Burg Metternich for views across fairy-tale Beilstein village.

TRY BOOTS OR BOATS: Hire a canoe or hike a section of the Moselsteig Trail for the journey between Bernkastel-Kues and Traben-Trarbach.

SAMPLE MOSELLE WINES: Visit at least one *Weingut*, to taste crisp whites and stock up for later.

NEED TO KNOW

Both ends of the Moselle Cycle Path are accessible by public transport: Perl is 35 minutes by bus from Luxembourg, Koblenz is 30 minutes from Bonn. Trier is an hour's train ride from Luxembourg (with connections to Brussels); frequent trains between Trier and Koblenz call at stations on or near the Moselle. Cruise boats also link some towns from April or May.

Left, from top: Moselle Cycle Path near Cochem; Reichsburg Castle, Cochem **Opposite:** Bernkastel-Kues

Estonia, Latvia & Lithuania

MAY–JUNE

SPRING BETWEEN STATES

● If you picture the Baltic States as a bit Dickensian – a tale of three cities – think again. Sure, the capitals' respective Old Towns are unmissable: Tallinn's medieval walled centre, the Gothic and baroque monuments of Vilnius, Rīga's Art Nouveau treasures. And sunny spring – after those cobblestoned streets have defrosted but before they ring with the footsteps of summer tour groups – is the time to discover their architectural and cultural wonders. But if you hopscotch straight between capitals, you'll miss countless unsung wonders: historic towns, traditional villages, beaches and bogs, forests, coast and islands across which wildflowers bloom now.

You could rent a car to scoot between highlights, from Vilnius to Kaunas' compact Old Town and 14th-century castle, coastal Klaipėda and the Curonian Spit. Then go from Rīga to Sigulda, for more castles and the caverns, forests and sandstone outcrops of Gauja National Park (home to elk, beavers, otters, wolves and bears). Head on through the strangely beautiful bogs of Soomaa National Park, Pärnu's white-sand beaches and the windswept pine groves of lovely Saaremaa Island, serene in pre-tourist season. But it's better to take it slow on the extensive public-transport system, or self-power your trip by cycling or hiking sections of the 3500km-plus (2175-mile) Baltic Trails network.

EXPERIENCES

SEE THE SPIT: Stroll the sands, pine stands and fishing villages of the Curonian Spit, the quirky finger of sand beckoning from Lithuania towards Kaliningrad.

PADDLE A PARK: Canoe the Gauja, Latvia's longest river, through its namesake national park, watching for deer, beavers and otters.

EXPLORE ARTSY TARTU: Estonia's unsung hip hangout is a cultured, lively student city with buzzing nightlife and magnificent neoclassical architecture.

GET CAPITAL: Don't miss those three big-hitters: Tallinn's turreted, walled Old Town; Vilnius' absorbing museums and 'independent' Užupis district; Rīga's century-spanning architectural marvels.

NEED TO KNOW

As you'd expect, southerly Lithuania tends to warm up before Estonia – average max temperatures for May are a couple of degrees higher in Vilnius than in Tallinn, where you can expect some chilly days even now. So if you're spending any length of time across the three Baltic States, safest to start in the south and work your way north rather than vice versa.

Left, from top: Gutman's Cave, Gauja National Park; Kayaking along the Gauja in Sigulda, Latvia **Opposite:** Blackheads House, Rīga

MAY

DRY SKIES, QUIETER SITES

Cuzco & the Sacred Valley, Peru

● The true offseason for Peru's Sacred Valley is January to February. These are the rainiest months, drenching everything and even, in February, officially closing some treks (including the Inca Trail). It's the cheapest time, yes, but is it worth it? Instead, wait it out until May. This is the start of the dry season, before the traditional holiday months of June to August when tourist numbers are most overwhelming, and securing permits for the Inca Trail is a bunfight (numbers are limited to 500 people per day, including guides and porters).

No, May is much mellower. Plus the landscapes are lush and the skies are increasingly clear. It's ideal for exploring the city of Cuzco, one-time capital of the vast Inca Empire, from its Qorikancha temple to its coffee bars. It's good for crowd-lite sightseeing along the Sacred Valley at Písac (host to a colourful thrice-weekly market) and the charming cobbled alleys of Ollantaytambo, dominated by a hillside fortress.

It's also good for hiking. The four-day Inca Trail is the classic, but you could lose any shoulder-season crowds by choosing an alternative route to Machu Picchu – such as the Choquequirao Trek, which traverses the mountains via an abandoned Inca city only accessible on foot.

EXPERIENCES

HAVE AN HISTORIC HIKE: The Inca Trail isn't only a terrific trek: it's the only way to see the en-route sites of Sayaqmarka, Phuyupatamarka or Wiñay Wayna.

TAKE A TRAIN: It's a scenic rail-ride from Poroy (near Cuzco) to Machu Picchu; the Cuzco–Puno train across the Andes to Lake Titicaca is another breathtaking option.

ADD THE AMAZON: From May to September, rainfall is lower, mosquitoes fewer and wildlife easier to glimpse.

WIND DOWN ON WATER: The outdoor centre at Laguna de Piuray, near Cuzco, offers responsible kayaking and SUP-ing, and a laid-back vibe.

NEED TO KNOW

Machu Picchu is open year-round. There's a daily cap on visitors: 5650 in high season (April–August), 4600 in low season. There are three visitor circuits; your ticket covers only the circuit you choose, not a full site exploration. A guide is mandatory. A separate ticket is required to climb the peaks of Wayna Picchu (150 tickets per day) and Huchuy Picchu (100 tickets per day).

Left, from top: Aboard the Cuzco–Puno train; Islas Uros, Lake Titicaca **Opposite:** Machu Picchu

Hawai‘i, USA

APRIL–MAY

LOW SEASON, BEST WEATHER

● Hawai‘i is the ultimate island paradise. Swaying palms, sugary sand, azure seas. Lush, dramatic and volcanic hinterlands. A reviving, vibrant culture. And year-round balminess: the mercury doesn't go much below 25°C (77°F) or above 30°C (86°F) here. What does change is the crowds. Peak times are December to February (winter escapees) and June to August (classic summer-holiday time). April to May though is especially dreamy: it's the start of the dry season, so you get great weather but fewer fellow tourists, and – as long as you avoid the Easter spike – way better prices and availability. You'll find laid-back beaches, hotel deals that won't blow your budget, and it'll be easier to snag a hire car. It's spring, too, so tropical fruits and flowers are running riot. You might also still spot the last of the humpback whales, which pass by from December to May.

Where to start? Pick your island carefully. Buzzy, family-friendly O‘ahu gets the most visitors by far. For a quieter mood, consider untamed Kaua‘i – top spot for hot hikes and waterfall chasing. Or Big Island, which is what it says on the tin: its supersized serving of rainforests, beaches and belching volcanoes means it's easy to lose the other people.

Left: Hanalei Bay, Kaua'i **Opposite:** Fish tacos at Kalapaki Beach, Kaua'i

EXPERIENCES

VISIT A VOLCANO: Big Island's Hawai'i Volcanoes National Park is home to Kīlauea and Mauna Loa, two of the archipelago's most active peaks.

EAT LOCAL: Tuck into island-grown apple-bananas and passionfruit, traditional *kālua pig* (shredded pork) and culinary-cultural mashups like spam sushi and fish tacos.

CATCH A BREAK: The swell calms a little in spring – it's a good time for beginners to try surfing.

HIT THE BEACH: Stellar shores include O'ahu's Kailua Bay, Kaua'i's handsome Hanalei Bay and Papakōlea on Big Island, for the chance to loll on green sand.

NEED TO KNOW

There are no ferries between the four main islands – hopping must be done by plane. You'll need at least five days per island, so if time is limited, stay on one. Cars are easier to hire in the offseason, when demand is lower. Buses run on Hawai'i's bigger islands, but other than on O'ahu, getting around by public transport is challenging.

Newfoundland, Canada

MAY–JUNE

IDEAL FOR ICEBERGS

● Poking into the ocean, on Canada's easternmost edge, Newfoundland has always lived at the whim of the North Atlantic. Its maritime climate isn't the kindest: traditionally it's seen as a summer destination; and July and August, when the weather is most reliably pleasant, are by far the busiest. At this time, as much tourist trade as possible is done – with prices hiked accordingly. But venture here outside those peak months and you'll be pleasantly surprised.

April–May is when great chunks of Arctic ice – mostly castoffs from the glaciers of western Greenland – start arriving in the province, drifting along the coast down what's known as 'Iceberg Alley'. Numbers of these glittering colossi tend to peak mid-May to June, floating away before summer begins. You can take a boat trip or watch them pass by from shore – prime lookouts include St Anthony, Bonavista, Cape Spear Lighthouse and the town of Twillingate. The latter is the best spot for kayaking amid growlers (the smallest chunks), bergy bits and gargantuan bergs the size of tower blocks. As a bonus, mid-May is when migrating whales start to show up; they hang around until mid-September. More than 20 species might be spotted, from humpbacks to minke, orca, sperm and blue.

EXPERIENCES

JOIN A KITCHEN PARTY: These traditional knees-ups see friends gather for informal jams and singalongs.

GO TO GROS MORNE: This national park is a wonderland of fjord-cut mountains and world-changing geology. The Trails, Tales and Tunes Festival is held here in the last two weeks of May in Norris Point.

ENJOY ST JOHN'S: The province's capital is a walkable, likeable, lively place to hang out.

WATCH BIRDS: Newfoundland is seabird central: Cape St Mary's Ecological Reserve (open early May to October) is a top spot; Elliston is excellent for puffins, which arrive mid-May.

NEED TO KNOW

Newfoundland's main airport is St John's International. The nearest airport to Gros Morne National Park is Deer Lake. Marine Atlantic ferries run year-round from North Sydney, Nova Scotia, to Newfoundland's Port aux Basques (a seven-hour crossing) and Argentia (16-hour crossing) terminals. Note that Newfoundland has its own time zone, which is 30 minutes ahead of Atlantic Standard Time.

Left, from top: Puffins, Bonavista; St John's **Opposite:** Twillingate's 'Iceberg Alley'

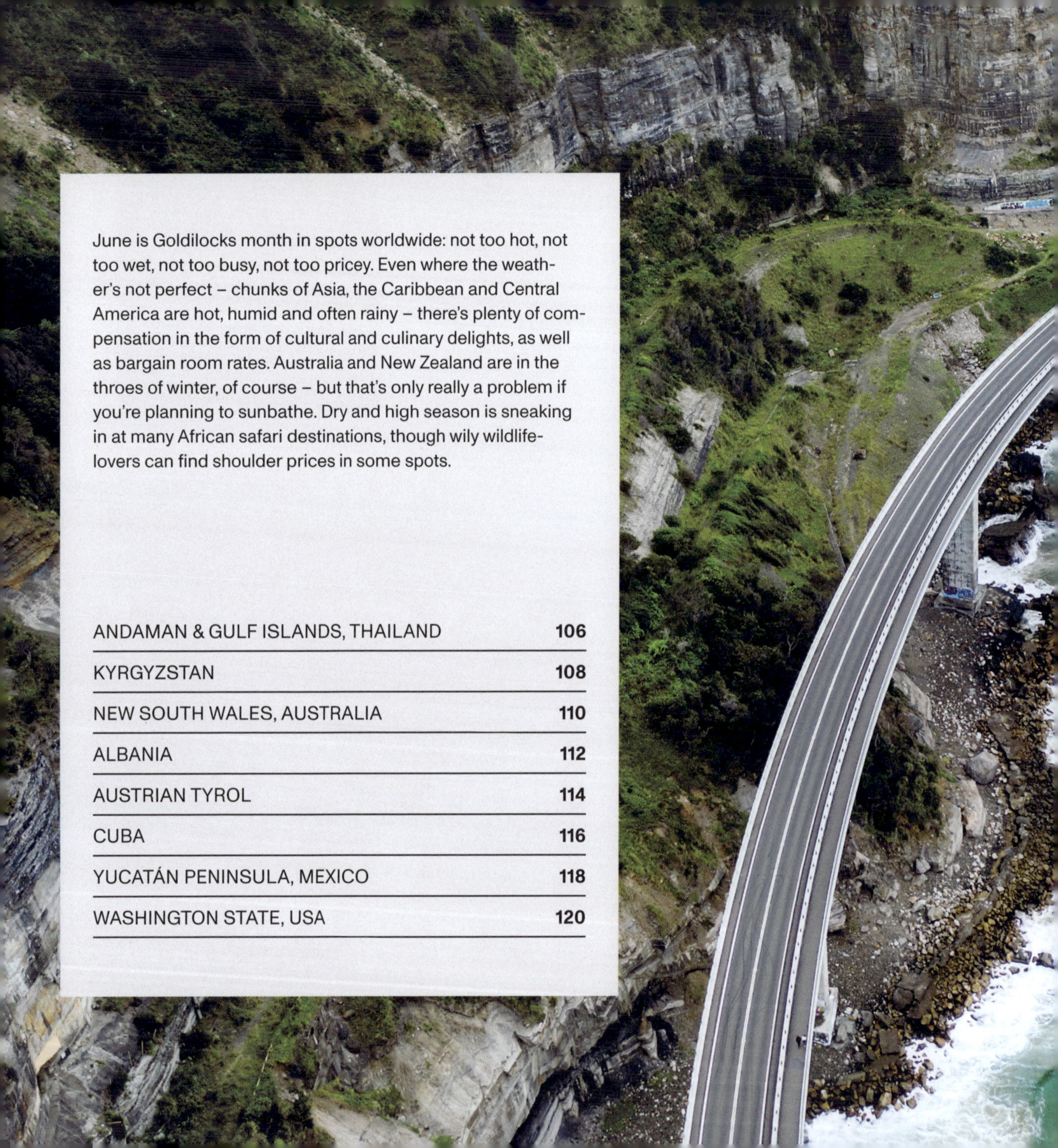

June is Goldilocks month in spots worldwide: not too hot, not too wet, not too busy, not too pricey. Even where the weather's not perfect – chunks of Asia, the Caribbean and Central America are hot, humid and often rainy – there's plenty of compensation in the form of cultural and culinary delights, as well as bargain room rates. Australia and New Zealand are in the throes of winter, of course – but that's only really a problem if you're planning to sunbathe. Dry and high season is sneaking in at many African safari destinations, though wily wildlife-lovers can find shoulder prices in some spots.

JUNE

Andaman & Gulf Islands, Thailand

MAY–JUNE

WETTER BUT QUIETER

● Received wisdom is head to Thailand from November to early April, when it's deliciously cool, dry and drop-dead gorgeous. But, of course, that's when everyone else goes. And this knock-out slice of Southeast Asia isn't diminished by a spot of rain. Especially in May and June, when downpours are less persistent than later in the wet season, and you can bag a whole lot of 30°C-plus (86°F) sunshine for half the price of peak time. You also have flexibility: the country's south is skinny, making it quick and easy to hop between the islands of the Andaman coast (on the west) and Gulf of Thailand (on the east), playing their different weather systems. The fact that there are fewer people about means accommodation doesn't need to be booked too far in advance, either.

The Gulf, home to popular Ko Samui, full-moon-party-famed Ko Pha-Ngan and laid-back Ko Tao, tends to be drier in general, and much quieter in this window before the European summer hols. The Andaman-side isles – diverse Phuket, cliff-craggy Krabi, cute Ko Lanta – can offer up excellent deals and a more relaxed feel. Plus, go with the right attitude and those storm clouds don't necessarily make things worse – just more atmospheric.

EXPERIENCES

COOK UP A STORM: If the weather's iffy, take a market tour then learn to make mouth-watering salads, punchy curries and hot-n-sour specialities – such as *tom yum koong* soup – in a local kitchen.

TAKE TO WATER: Pick a calm day to boat-trip the karst outcrops of Phuket's Phang Nga Bay or around pristine Ang Thong Marine National Park.

WANDER TO WATERFALLS: After a bout of rain, Thailand's cascades will be in full flow.

BAG A BEACH: In low season you might get some sand to yourself; Ko Lanta has excellent isolated spots.

NEED TO KNOW

Low-cost flights link Bangkok to resorts such as Ko Samui and Phuket. Alternatively, use cheap long-distance buses (Bangkok–Phuket, 12 hours). Do your research before booking a beach stay. Some of Thailand's coastal resorts have become extremely overdeveloped, with high-rises, rowdy bars and dubious water quality ruining the paradise vibes – once-idyllic Ko Phi-Phi, for example, is now depressingly overloved. Look elsewhere.

Left, from top: Spectacled langur, Ko Wua Ta Lap, Ang Thong Marine National Park; Spicy *tom yum koong* soup **Opposite:** Ko Pha-Ngan

Kyrgyzstan

JUNE

PRE-PEAK PEAKS

● The Switzerland of Central Asia, you say? Well, that's the word on the Bishkek street. Not that the word's got out very far. Because though Kyrgyzstan's two mighty ranges – the Tien Shan, soaring to 7439m-high (24,406ft) Pobeda Peak on the Chinese border, and the Pamir Mountains – justify that moniker, few international visitors make it here. For most of the year, this former Soviet republic is chilly and lonely, with winter riming snowy swathes from November into March or April. Things only heat up in July and August, when flights and accommodation are pricier and often booked solid.

By June, many mountain trails and nomad *ger* (yurt) camps offering insights into nomadic lifestyles are open – though very high-altitude paths may still be snowed under, and you'll want to bring warm layers for chilly nights among the peaks. Capital Bishkek and the lush Fergana Valley are pleasant, hitting around 25°C (77°F) but not yet steaming, while idyllic Issyk-Köl beckons hardy lake-swimmers.

June's also ideal for roaming the verdant forested valleys that notch the Tien Shan, south of Karakol. Add walnut forests around the mountain village of Arslanbob, the striking sandstone cliffs of Jeti-Ögüz and more shimmering lakes like Song-Köl, remote Köl-Suu and turquoise Köl-Tör, and your adventure plan writes itself.

Left: Altyn-Arashan *ger* camp **Opposite:** Osh Bazaar, Bishkek

EXPERIENCES

SADDLE UP FOR SONG-KÖL: Ride across the steppe to reach this loveliest of lakes on horseback, enjoying the light dancing on surrounding peaks.

BROWSE OSH BAZAAR: Delve into Bishkek's huge central market to pick up fresh seasonal fruits, musical instruments or maybe a traditional felt *ak kalpak* hat.

HIKE ALTYN-ARASHAN: Set out from Karakol to explore this comely mountain valley, easing muscles afterwards with a dunk in its natural hot springs.

COOL OFF IN ISSYK-KÖL: Take a brisk dip in the world's second-largest alpine lake, or grab a paddle to kayak its sparkling waters.

NEED TO KNOW

Getting to Kyrgyzstan's main gateway, Bishkek, typically involves flying via an intermediate hub, İstanbul being the most convenient for travellers from Europe or North America. Vegetarians and vegans, be warned: Kyrgyz cuisine is seriously meat-heavy, with mutton in most dishes – tell hotels, guesthouses, *ger* camps and homestay owners in advance if you need meat-free food. September's another quieter month to visit.

JUNE–JULY

WARM WINTER ROAD-TRIPPING

New South Wales, Australia

● Honestly, it IS winter in New South Wales, but put on a jacket and you'd barely notice. Highs of 'only' around 16°C (61°F) are certainly no reason to bypass always-spirited Sydney for a few days – its hotels are so much cheaper at this time of year – and then head south on a road trip (car hire will also cost less).

There are many epic routes you could take. But the Grand Pacific Drive, which hugs the coast down to Jervis Bay, is a beaut. From Sydney, it's only 205km (127 miles), but going small and slow, and lingering in the little places, suits a season when locals will have more time to chat. Plus there's plenty to see along the way.

Stop off to explore the rugged shores and eucalyptus bush of Royal National Park – between June and August whales might be spotted from the 26km (16-mile) Bundeena to Otford coastal hiking route. Drive across the spectacular 665m-long (2182ft) Sea Cliff Bridge. Soak up the cosy bookshop-and-cafe culture of hangouts like Austinmer and Wollongong. And seek out hallowed surf beaches like Farm and Mystics – from June to August, low-pressure systems in the Tasman Sea create solid swells, making this the best surf season.

EXPERIENCES

SEE CINEMA: The Sydney Film Festival, held at the art deco State Theatre, runs over two weeks in June.

GO ZEN: The Nan Tien Temple, near Wollongong, is the largest Buddhist temple in the southern hemisphere; it has a Pilgrim Lodge offering overnight stays.

WALK AT BASS POINT: This reserve is one of the most important archaeological sites on the New South Wales coast; the self-guided Indigenous Cultural Walk reveals the history.

WATCH WHALES: Humpbacks migrate along the coast in winter; take a whale-spotting boat trip (May–November) from ports such as Shellharbour.

NEED TO KNOW

Allow two to five days for the Grand Pacific Drive. From Jervis Bay you could continue south to the Victoria border along the scenic Sapphire Coast. Alternatively, return to Sydney via the Southern Highlands, which will be cool and frosty – perfect for bracing bushwalks and warming up afterwards with a glass of local Shiraz or Pinot Noir.

Left, from top: Wollongong; Sydney's Maroubra Beach **Opposite:** Sea Cliff Bridge, Grand Pacific Drive

Albania

APRIL–EARLY JUNE

PEAKS AND PAST GLORIES

● Once a Cold War pariah notorious for its paranoia and isolation, today Albania is hot property – scorching, in fact, if you come in high summer, when its long, golden Mediterranean beaches are thronged. Don't. Instead, spring for balmier April, May and early June, when you can lounge on those sandy strands in relative peace. But do make time to explore the historical and natural wonders of this diverse land, with attractions and accommodation also quieter and often cheaper in these mellow months.

Capital Tirana's a vibrant hotchpotch, mixing Italian, Ottoman and Communist-era architecture with hip cafes, hopping bars and hyped street art, all best enjoyed in warm spring sunshine. Up north, the so-called Accursed Mountains – or Albanian Alps – form a natural barrier with Montenegro. Now's the time to take to the trails, hiking between homestays in rural villages such as Theth, with its fortified lockup tower. The eastern border with North Macedonia bisects Lake Ohrid – hop across to the namesake town, with its medieval basilica and nearby Sveti Naum Monastery.

Then head south for some history: crag-top castles and fascinating throwback Ottoman houses in Berat and Gjirokastra; medieval art and a buzzing 500-year-old bazaar in Korça; and ancient, UNESCO-listed Butrint, just a short hop from those southern beaches.

EXPERIENCES

DISCOVER HIGHLAND LIFE: Hike the 'Accursed' Albanian Alps through forested valleys and across high passes between traditional villages like Theth and Valbona.

FIND FOOD FOR FORT: Sample local dishes in restaurants flanking limestone-flagged streets, then explore the castle and fortified Ottoman houses of hilltop Gjirokastra.

GO GREEK: Explore the astonishing archaeological remains of Hellenic-Roman-Venetian Butrint, roaming its ancient acropolis, theatre, bathhouses and palace.

NAB A BEACH SPOT: The sandy strands and balmy waters of the Albanian Riviera in the southwest beckon before the crowds descend later in June.

NEED TO KNOW

Temperatures soar from late June, topping 30°C (86°F) through July and August, particularly in the lowlands and south – pretty unbearable in cities like Tirana, driving locals and tourists alike to beach resorts such as Saranda and Ksamil. If you come in May or early June, consider heading to quieter, more northerly beaches around Himara and Dhërmi.

Left, from top: Theth, Accursed Mountains; Ksamil, Albanian Riviera **Opposite:** Palace of Culture, Tirana

Austrian Tyrol

MAY–JUNE

THE HILLS ARE ALIVE

● Painted on the vast canvas of the Alps, June is the Tyrol's blue period. Above, clear skies reflected in clear tarns; below, meadows carpeted with profusely blooming gentians.

Not so profuse at this time of year are tourists. While snow's melting on high trails, and mountain huts are opening their shutters for the season, only a handful of in-the-know hikers and mountain-lovers arrive to admire the floral displays; the masses won't descend till July (and again during ski season, of course), keeping down costs as well as crowds.

In June, you won't have selfie-snappers photobombing your shots of Innsbruck's Aldstadt (Old Town) – the Habsburg dynasty's Hofburg (imperial palace); Hofkirche and Goldenes Dachl (Golden Roof), its 2657 gilded copper shingles installed at the turn of the 16th century. You won't be jostling for space on the 24,000km (14,913 miles) of marked hiking trails, or while forest-bathing in the beech and spruce woods, tackling singletrack mountain-bike trails, or spotting chamois, ibex, marmots and eagles. Not in the pristine lakes, spas and pools, or at the fairy-tale medieval castles guarding towns, passes and valleys: the burly stone tower of 13th-century Schloss Landeck, the polygonal Münzerturm (Mint Tower) of Burg Hasegg, and hulking Festung (Fortress) Kufstein.

EXPERIENCES

HIKE THE HEIGHTS: Tackle the Stubai Höhenweg, one of the great Alpine multiday routes, trekking between cosy mountain huts.

ADMIRE INNSBRUCK: Discover Renaissance palaces, Gothic and Baroque churches, museums and glittering Goldenes Dachl.

ENJOY WATERY WELLNESS: Relax in one of the Tyrol's many excellent spas; take some Kneipp water therapy; swim in one of many Alpine lakes – or just cool off under a mountain waterfall.

ADRENALINE RUSH: Up the ante with a high-speed ride on a summer toboggan or coaster run, flying-fox zip-line or high-ropes course.

NEED TO KNOW

Planning to stay in some of the region's characterful mountain huts? Join the Österreichischer Alpenverein (Austrian Alpine Club) for chunky discounts on stays and food at more than 200 huts across Austria, Germany and Italian South Tyrol. Some have private rooms; in others you'll bed down in Matratzenlager (large dorms with tightly packed mattresses). They typically open from mid-June.

Left, from top: Schlegeis Stausee from the Olpererhütte suspension bridge; Innsbruck's Hofkirche **Opposite:** Aldstadt, Innsbruck

MAY–JUNE

COOL CARIBBEAN HEAT

Cuba

● Cuba is a land apart. It's kissed by the same sultry breezes as the rest of the Caribbean, but is utterly unlike it. It's only 140km (87 miles) from the USA as the trogon flies, but a million miles away ideologically. Geographically, it's relatively small but – from its pulsating beats to its heady cocktails, fat cigars and Che Guevara T-shirts – it's a cultural giant.

Simply, Cuba is hot, in every sense. And particularly right now. May and June are the start of the wetter, warmer season, with rain increasingly likely, temperatures pushing 30°C (86°F) and numbers of visitors way down. But it's before things start getting really sticky and stormy (that happens August to October), so if you're willing to risk getting a bit wet, there are bargains and empty beaches to be found.

It's a particularly good time to explore places that are usually crowded: the limestone mountains and tobacco plantations of the Viñales Valley, or Santa Clara (home to Che's striking mausoleum). Then there's the spirited city of Santiago de Cuba and hypnotic Havana, the gloriously crumbling capital, with all its vintage cars and mojito bars. The best plan? Spend mornings adventuring – maybe a hike in the Sierra del Escambray – and hot afternoons chilling beside the turquoise sea.

EXPERIENCES

SEEK OUT A STOGIE: Lush Viñales Valley is where the world's best dark tobacco is processed into its finest cigars; see them made in situ.

LEARN TO (SON) DANCE: The infectious *son* rhythms at Trinidad's Casa de la Trova cultural centre will have even novices busting some moves.

HAVE A HISTORIC DRINK: El Floridita in Havana was a favourite of Hemingway's, who came here to drink daiquiris.

HIT THE BEACH: Tropical paradise can be found at spots like laid-back Cayo Levisa, picture-perfect Cayo las Brujas and dazzling Santa María del Mar, near the capital.

NEED TO KNOW

Casas particulares are private houses where locals open a few guest rooms to tourists. They are basic, with fans (not air-con) and sometimes shared rather than en-suite bathrooms. However, they tend to be clean, friendly and a great way to get a better insight into Cuban culture. Hosts often don't speak much English – packing a phrasebook and learning some lingo will be helpful.

Left, from top: Cigar making, Viñales Valley; Santa María del Mar, Havana **Opposite:** Havana

Yucatán Peninsula, Mexico

MAY–JUNE

HISTORY AND HEAT

● What's that throaty rumble? That'll be Chaac, Maya god of rain and thunder, thwacking bulbous storm clouds with his lightning axe. It's a sound you'll quickly get used to in the Yucatán now. Because Chaac – aka, the wet season – is wielding a firm grip on this heartland of the ancient civilisation that flourished here some 2500 years ago. And that's not such a bad thing.

Dry weather dominates November to April, bringing clear seas – and tourists. By July, downpours – sometimes hurricanes – have arrived in earnest, though that doesn't deter many summer visitors, either. But these first rainy months see mostly afternoon storms that help dissipate the humidity and heat (highs average around 33°C/91°F) as well as the crowds that later throng Tulum's white-sand beaches and incredible ancient sites like Chichén Itzá, with its ball courts, reclining Chac Mool stone figures and monumental temples. Prices are low, availability high, and the history, natural beauty and wildlife more easily enjoyed in peace.

Whale sharks cruise past the coast from June, while green and loggerhead turtles lumber ashore to dig nests and lay eggs. Vibrant towns such as walled Campeche and 'White City' Mérida hum with markets and music. And in the emerald forests, the distinctive water-filled limestone sinkholes called cenotes beckon alluringly – instant cool.

EXPERIENCES

ABSORB ANCIENT HISTORY: Explore the remains of Maya cities – epic Chichén Itzá, jungle-swaddled Calakmul, beautiful Uxmal, rainforest-clad Cobá.

EMBRACE RESTING BEACH FACE: Chill on the sandy shores of Tulum, with its spectacular clifftop Maya ruins; or Isla Cozumel, famed for great snorkelling and diving.

GO WILD: Explore Reserva de la Biosfera Sian Ka'an, a vast swathe of tropical forests, mangroves and reefs, watching for spider and howler monkeys, nesting turtles, tapirs, dazzling birdlife and even jaguars.

MEET THE MAYA: Stay in a traditional Maya community to learn about ancient customs and timeless lifestyles.

NEED TO KNOW

The Tren Maya or Tsíimin K'áak is a 1554km-long (966-mile) train route completed at the end of 2024. Consisting of two linked lines running between Cancún and Palenque, it connects popular tourist hubs such as Tulum and Playa del Carmen with Mérida, Campeche and many key Maya ruins – including Chichén Itzá and more off-the-beaten-track sites like Calakmul.

Left, from top: Cenote Ik Kil, near Chichén Itzá; Mérida **Opposite:** Tulum

Washington State, USA

JUNE

JUST BEFORE THE CROWDS

● The weather in Washington State is pretty reliable – that is, reliably wet. This chunk of the Pacific Northwest, especially on the western side of the Cascade Range, gets a lot of rain, year-round. The best bet? Come in June and keep your fingers crossed. July and August are the driest, warmest and busiest months to experience this magisterial region; in June, you might luck out on similar weather, but with a fraction of the crowds – just pack a waterproof.

Late spring comes with other benefits, too; like peak summer, it's one of the best months for camping trips and hikes. In Olympic National Park – a vast wilderness of glacier-licked peaks, ancient temperate rainforest and untamed Pacific shores – some roads, camp-grounds and other facilities are closed from October through May; by June, everything is open, and ranger-led activities – from nature walks to stargazing – recommence.

And it's one of the best times for whales; species such as humpback, minke, fin and orca might be spotted. You might even see the latter, hunting for salmon, from kayak-level on a paddle around the state's spectacular San Juan Islands.

EXPERIENCES

LIGHT UP THE NIGHT: After-dark kayaking around the San Juan Islands can deliver a phantasmagoria of bioluminescent plankton; June–August is best due to abundant sunlight and warmer waters.

HAVE A HOT CUPPA: The state's proliferation of coffee micro-roasters means there's always a great brew nearby.

SAUNTER THE SHORE: Wave-battered, wild Ruby Beach on Olympic Peninsula is perfect for bracing walks in all weathers.

MARVEL AT MT RAINIER: The magnificent national park encompassing this 4392m-high (14,410ft), glacier-dripped stratovolcano is heaving in high summer; explore before the masses arrive.

NEED TO KNOW

Washington is served by three Amtrak trains: the Empire Builder (Chicago to Seattle), Coast Starlight (LA to Seattle) and Amtrak Cascades (Vancouver to Eugene, Oregon). Extensive Washington State Ferries services include Anacortes (a two- to three-hour drive from Seattle) to the San Juan Islands. A seasonal surcharge is added to ferry tickets for travel between May and late September.

Left, from top: Kayaking, Deer Harbor, San Juan Islands; Ruby Beach, Olympic National Park **Opposite:** Reflection Lakes, Mt Rainier National Park

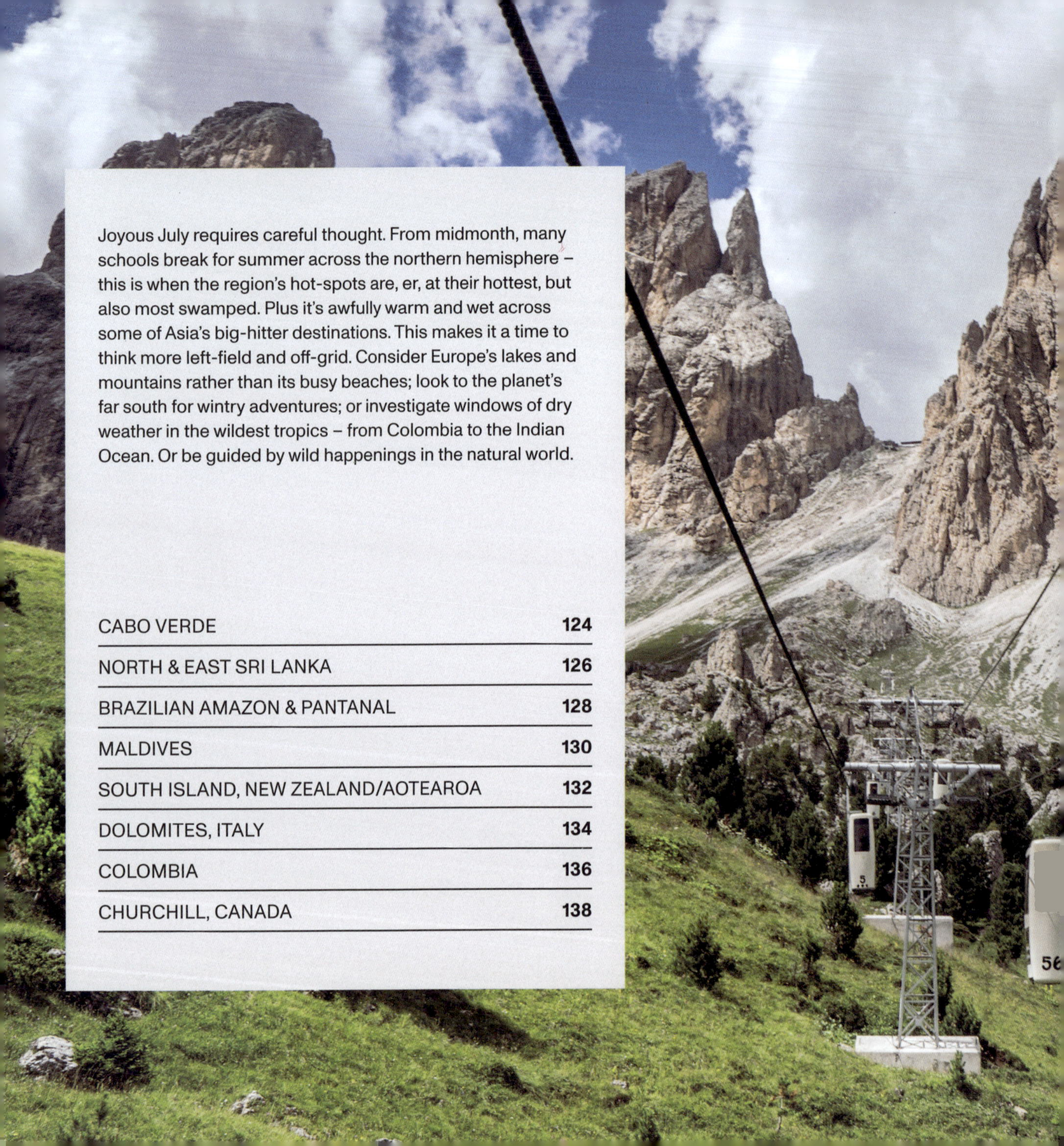

Joyous July requires careful thought. From midmonth, many schools break for summer across the northern hemisphere – this is when the region's hot-spots are, er, at their hottest, but also most swamped. Plus it's awfully warm and wet across some of Asia's big-hitter destinations. This makes it a time to think more left-field and off-grid. Consider Europe's lakes and mountains rather than its busy beaches; look to the planet's far south for wintry adventures; or investigate windows of dry weather in the wildest tropics – from Colombia to the Indian Ocean. Or be guided by wild happenings in the natural world.

JULY

JUNE–JULY

WET(ISH) BUT WORTH IT

Cabo Verde

● Adrift off the coast of West Africa, the 10-island archipelago of Cabo Verde was forged by undersea volcanics, shaped by the trade in enslaved people and once ruled by Portugal. Now it sways to its own infectious beat – though it remains at the mercy of the Atlantic Ocean. Yes, it can be crazily windy, brutally dry and occasionally dusty (with sand clouds blown in from the Sahara here) – but also tropically lush, deliciously warm and beautifully sunny. For freezing northern Europeans, it's a popular winter-sun retreat, especially the beaches of family-friendly Sal and laid-back Boa Vista. But there's no reason not to opt for summer instead.

June to July is increasingly hot, and officially the start of the 'rainy' season – though in reality, July's rainfall register is only around 10mm (0.4in). It's still lovely for lounging by warm waves, especially as the winds have dropped.

This is also a good time for exploring further afield. Santiago, the main isle, is the place for history – Cabo Verde's only UNESCO site, the old Portuguese city of Cidade Velha, is here. Santo Antão is the hikers' island, with varied trails via lush valleys, wild shores and barren plateaus. For culture, head to Mindelo on São Vicente, birthplace of legendary singer Cesária Évora and home to many live-music bars.

Left, from top: Pico do Fogo, Fogo; Paúl Valley, Santo Antão **Opposite:** Cidade Velha, Santiago

EXPERIENCES

DASH TO THE DUNES: Boa Vista has some spectacular sands, including Praia de Chaves, a long, golden sweep that merges into lunar-like dunes.

HIKE SANTO ANTÃO: Top routes include the trek up the verdant Paúl Valley, or along the wild north coast past the rainbow-hued, ridge-teetering village of Fontainhas.

RAISE A GLASS: Fogo is home to Pico do Fogo, Cabo Verde's only active volcano, and the island's rich, dark soil is good for grapes; try the Chã das Caldeiras white.

SEE TURTLES: Loggerheads nest on Boa Vista and Sal between June and October.

NEED TO KNOW

There are international airports on Santiago, São Vicente, Sal and Boa Vista. Internal flights and ferries connect the islands, though delays and cancellations are common – complex island-hopping itineraries are not recommended. A notable exception is the pretty reliable hourlong ferry between São Vicente and Santo Antão. Taxis and *aluguers* (shared taxis) are the main modes of transport on the islands.

North & East Sri Lanka

MAY–AUGUST

THE NON-MONSOON SIDE

● No matter when you visit this Indian Ocean isle, it'll be toasty hot. Sri Lanka dangles just above the equator, with highs around 30°C (86°F) year-round; the welcome from the local people, renowned for their hospitality, is always warm, too. But it's an island of two halves, rain-wise, with monsoons dumping on different regions at different times.

Sri Lanka's peak season – December to March – is when it's driest in the popular south and west. But visit when the Yala Monsoon hits those areas from May to August and you'll find a quieter, cheaper paradise isle. At this time it makes sense to head to the lesser-visited north and east, where the weather stays dry and the crowds are always thinner. Take in the culture-rich cities of Jaffna and Trincomalee, the latter a great spot for watching blue and sperm whales – they congregate to mate in Trinco's natural harbour between June and October.

Venture down the east coast, hopping between laid-back villages like Arugam Bay, where consistent swells make for a good place to go to surf school. And add on a trip to Wilpattu National Park, where the dry weather makes the animals – Asian elephants, sambar deer, sloth bears, leopards – easier to spot.

Left: Elephant, Minneriya National Park **Opposite:** Trincomalee

EXPERIENCES

OGLE ELEPHANTS: The annual 'Gathering' of 300-or-so elephants at Minneriya National Park occurs from July to September.

GRAB A SNORKEL: The paradisiacal Pigeon Island Marine Sanctuary, near Trincomalee, has Sri Lanka's best coral and is a turtle hot-spot; waters are clearest May to September.

EXPLORE JAFFNA: Delve into Tamil culture, visit the huge Nallur Kandaswamy Kovil Hindu temple and tour the fort, variously held through history by the Portuguese, Dutch and British.

ISLAND-HOP: Ferries and causeways link the scatter of slow-paced isles west of Jaffna; slowest is Neduntheevu (aka Delft), where wild horses roam.

NEED TO KNOW

Trains run from Colombo to Jaffna (six to seven hours) and Colombo to Trincomalee (eight hours). Third class can be uncomfortably cramped. Reserved second-class seats offer more space and windows that open for cooling breezes and better views and photos; first class is a bit plusher, with air-conditioning, but you can't open the windows. Tickets can be booked online or at stations.

Brazilian Amazon & Pantanal

JUNE–JULY

WILD TIMES

● Best time to be in Brazil? It's complicated. For one thing, Latin America's largest country is a behemoth: at over 8.5 million sq km (3.28 million sq miles), Brazil is bigger than the USA's contiguous 48, and occupies a full half of its continent. Stretching some 4350km (2700 miles) from east to west and north to south, it spans four time zones and the equator. When it's winter in the south, the Brazilian Amazon is...well, a bit drier, but no cooler. And when it's hot in Rio from December to February, it's raining, too. But also busiest with tourists and generally pricier. Confused, much?

Where to go and when depends what you're looking for – and if that means smaller crowds (away from beaches) but big cats, kaleidoscopic birds, river dolphins, caiman and capybara, July's a good shout. On a Rio Negro river cruise from Manaus, water levels are typically ebbing, exposing beaches and walking trails (though you may also traverse different types of wildlife-rich flooded forest known as *igapó* and *várzea*); aquatic creatures (including dolphins) can also be easier to spot.

Meanwhile, down in the Pantanal – the world's largest tropical wetland – receding waters make for spectacular wildlife-watching: birds and reptiles cluster at pools, and jaguars hunt capybara on riverbanks.

EXPERIENCES

CRUISE THE RIO NEGRO: Board a riverboat in Manaus to explore one of the Amazon's most impressive tributaries, watching for mating caiman, profuse birdlife, and tucuxi and boto river dolphins.

TRACK GIANTS IN THE PANTANAL: Encounter the oversized species of the world's largest wetland, including the Americas' biggest cat (the jaguar), plus giant river otters and anteaters, tapirs and capybara.

GET CULTURED: Discover the museums, galleries and cultural marvels of Manaus, catching a performance at the extraordinary Teatro Amazonas opera house.

NEED TO KNOW

Schools in Brazil are on holiday in July, so beaches can be crowded. While this is typically the early drier season in the Amazon, climate change is disrupting rainfall patterns, making seasons and water levels less predictable. By July, forests may still be flooded – or walking trails may already be largely accessible. Whatever the conditions, you'll be immersed in nature – just in slightly different ways.

Left, from top: Capybara and cowbird, Pantanal; Teatro Amazonas, Manaus **Opposite:** Amazon river taxi between Manaus and Careiro da Várzea

Maldives

MAY–AUGUST

LOWER-PRICED PARADISE

● The thousand-plus coral isles of the Maldives lie sprinkled across the Indian Ocean, upwards of the equator. It's never really chilly or less than paradise here: the beaches are always dazzling and palm-y, the seas blue and balmy. That said, most visitors come in the drier months (December to April), seeking clearer skies and cooling breezes – and finding higher prices. May to August is a much cheaper time to play castaway. You'll get a little more rain but still plenty of sunshine (downpours tend to be short). Note, southern atolls tend to see more rain than northern ones.

The stormier season does riffle the seas, but that means it's the best time for taking lessons at one of the Maldives' surf schools – waves are biggest June to July. And while the plankton bloom that occurs at this time means diving visibility is slightly reduced, it means more big creatures come to feast: July and August are great times for finning with manta rays and whale sharks in the South Ari and Baa Atolls.

There's also a bit of a party vibe: 26 July is Maldives Independence Day, when parades and performances are held, more cultural activities are on offer and traditional dishes are cooked up and shared.

EXPERIENCES

GO LOCAL: Many Maldivian islands are home to local communities with homestay-style accommodation rather than resorts – try Maafushi (connected to Malé by ferry) and Fulhadhoo, on Baa Atoll.

GET CRAFTY: If it's raining, join an art class, take a Maldivian drum lesson, try thatch-roof-making or learn some words of local dialect Dhivehi bas.

DO SOME CITIZEN SCIENCE: Several resorts partner with conservation organisations; you can record data on boat trips and dives that help research.

SAFARI UNDERSEA: There's good snorkelling nationwide, but Baa Atoll's Hanifaru Lagoon is an idyllic soup of sea creatures.

NEED TO KNOW

The Maldives' main airport is Malé's Velana International. Domestic scheduled flights connect to islands with airports, with onward transfers usually made by speedboat. Velana International also has a seaplane terminal – the most fun, luxurious and expensive way to travel. Slow, cheap public ferries serve local islands, but not resort islands; most of these ferries don't operate on Fridays.

Left, from top: Making traditional mats; Hawksbill turtle, Hanifaru Lagoon **Opposite:** Mas huni, a typical breakfast dish

South Island, New Zealand/Aotearoa

JUNE–AUGUST

WHITE, WATER, WHALES

● The beautiful south hits different in winter. There's more snow than sun, that's for sure. Powderhounds come to carve pistes at Craigieburn, Mt Olympus and Treble Cone, while beginners play nice at Cardrona. But the thrills don't stop with skiing. Hurtle downhill on a toboggan, mush your own dogsled team or try a snowshoe expedition – a guided excursion, or an overnight or multiday adventure to experience the inky blackness of the night sky above the Southern Alps and a widescreen stargazing show. It's not all drifts and downhills, though – away from the slopes, in particular, visitor numbers plummet and there are midwinter deals to be had.

Head to the east coast and Kaikōura, where the namesake mountain ranges provide a spectacular backdrop for the breaching, fin-slapping humpback whales that cruise this stretch of coast between June and August.

And though most Great Walks are effectively off-menu over winter, with hut facilities pared right back and trail conditions treacherous in Fiordland and Mt Aspiring National Parks, you can still experience fine hiking. Tracing the fractal shore of the island's far north, the 60km (37-mile) Abel Tasman Coast Track is alluring year-round, with golden beaches, lush forests and wildlife – watch for playful fur seals and rare kākā parrots, and listen for the melodious songs of bellbirds/korimako.

EXPERIENCES

SNOWSHOE THE SLOPES: Join a guided adventure into the hills above Wānaka; the Remarkables from Queenstown; or the Southern Alps from Lake Tekapo/Takapō.

STROLL THE SHORE: Hike some or all of the Abel Tasman Coast Track over three to five days, camping or staying in huts en route.

WATCH WHALES: Board a whale-watching boat from Kaikōura or, better still, kayak among fur seals, keeping eyes peeled for albatross and migrating humpback whales.

WARM UP IN HOT SPRINGS: Plunge into the warm waters of a natural hot spring – maybe Maruia or Hanmer Springs.

NEED TO KNOW

Though winter is generally low season here, ski resorts – and Queenstown in particular – can get busy, especially during Australian and New Zealand school holidays, which typically span the first two or three weeks of July. If you plan to ski, book ahead or come later in the month (or in August). Alternatively, base yourself somewhere quieter – Wānaka or Mt Hutt, for example.

Left, from top: Abel Tasman Coast Track near Mārahau; sperm whale offshore of Kaikōura **Opposite:** Hiking near Wānaka

Dolomites, Italy

JUNE–JULY

SNOW-FREE, STILL COOL

● Europe's most beautiful mountains? They just might be. The divine Dolomites guard northern Italy, a craggy bulwark of towers, turrets and spires rising from rippling plateaus, with a tendency to flush pink-purple at sunset – a dreamy phenomenon called the *enrosadira*. Skiers are well-versed in their winter charms: Dolomiti Superski, with 1246km (774 miles) of pistes across 12 resorts, is the world's largest ski area. But fewer people have cottoned on to the UNESCO-listed range's spring-to-summer charms, when the valleys are wildflower-bright and cow-grazed, the forests are a lush green and the slopes attract far fewer people – especially in June and the first weeks of July, before schools kick out.

Providing respite from the scorching heat that can incapacitate other parts of Europe at this time, the Dolomites have everything required for a glorious mild-weather adventure. There are hundreds of kilometres of cycle paths, hiking trails and via ferrata, accessible via cable cars and efficient public transport. There's intriguing history, from Ladin culture (which has existed here for millennia) to remnants of WWI, when these peaks became a battlefield. And there's some of the best food you'll ever eat, from Michelin-starred menus served in mountain huts to fresh-from-the-pasture cheeses.

EXPERIENCES

FOLLOW AN 'IRON ROAD': The use of via ferrata was pioneered here by WWI troops; some historic routes can still be traversed.

GET ON YOUR BIKE: Try the 30km (19-mile) Dobbiaco–Cortina route, which uses an old railway line but offers big views; or the 105km (65-mile) Pustertal path, which hops into Austria.

LIVE LADIN: Alta Badia's Nos Ladins programme offers an introduction to this unique culture via experiences with local farmers, cooks and artisans.

HIKE THE HILLS: So many options. The 120km (75-mile) Alta Via 1 is a classic hut-to-hut trek.

NEED TO KNOW

Held in the first week of July, and starting from La Villa in Alta Badia, the Maratona dles Dolomites is billed as one of the world's largest and most chaotic cycling events. This one-day road-bike race, taking in seven passes, is open to amateurs; during the preceding 'Riders' Week', training events and parties are held daily, and the area gets very busy.

Left: Lago di Carezza **Opposite:** Bocchette via ferrata

JULY–SEPTEMBER

STEAMY AND SENSATIONAL

Colombia

● Caribbean beaches, Amazon rainforest, Andes mountains. Ancient monuments, Spanish-era cities, volcanic hills striped with coffee plantations. Whales in the Pacific, giant anteaters on the Los Llanos plains, dazzling birds among the peaks. Colombia's a true travel variety pack: a dizzying smorgasbord of experiences and sights spread across numerous landscapes and regions – with diverse climates to boot.

Driest months overall are December to March, when crowds and costs rise. Insider tip: there's a midyear window between the soggiest months – a mini July–August dry season when you can exploit better conditions and often rather lower prices. Sure, you can't dodge rain entirely – but then that's true at any time in this tropical equatorial nation. And July brings other compensations: humpback whales arrive off the Pacific coast, downpours start easing in the highlands, and carnivals come to central Colombia. Bogotá's Summer Festival is packed with culture, art and sport; Villa de Leyva celebrates the Fiesta de la Virgen del Carmen with parades and dances; and Medellín's streets blaze with blooms during its Flower Festival from month's end.

Rain or not, you can't miss the sultry vibes of Cartagena – explore in peace, ending your day with cocktails as the sun sets into the Caribbean for total tropical utopia.

EXPERIENCES

WANDER COLOURFUL CARTAGENA: Roam the walled Old Town of this Caribbean port city, founded in 1533 by the Spanish.

WATCH WHALES: Witness humpbacks cruise along Colombia's Pacific coast from July to November.

BOOST YOUR CAFFEINE LEVELS: Tour coffee fincas (plantations) in the Zona Cafetera amid pretty Spanish-style villages, rolling emerald hills and active volcanoes, making time to hike the Cocora Valley.

GO WILD: Explore Parque Nacional Natural Tayrona's beaches and wildlife-packed jungle, or join a group for the six-day trek through lush tropical forests to the ancient Ciudad Perdida (Lost City).

NEED TO KNOW

Though a ceasefire called time on the half-century-long FARC insurgency in 2016, attacks and kidnappings by various groups may present a threat in some areas. Check travel advice from your government's foreign office or equivalent, and avoid regions designated as risky. The Pacific whale-watching hubs of Nuquí and Bahía Solano are typically safe, though surrounding areas may be considered problematic.

Left, from top: Humpback whale offshore of Nuquí; Ciudad Perdida, Santa Marta **Opposite:** Plaza de los Coches, Cartagena

Churchill, Canada

JULY

WHITE BEARS, WHITE WHALES

● Stranded on the shores of Hudson Bay, on the 58th parallel north, Churchill, Manitoba, is an isolated spot. And yet considerable numbers of people make pilgrimages here, keen to visit the 'Polar Bear Capital of the World'. Every year a thousand or so of the huge animals migrate here to hunt for seals. Perceived wisdom is that the best months to see them are October and November, when the bears gather by the lake, waiting for the waters to freeze so they can hunt on the ice. At this time fat-wheeled buggies take travellers onto the tundra for close encounters – advance booking is essential.

But the bears begin migrating to Churchill from July – it's not uncommon to see them wandering about in the longer, warmer days of summer, rolling around in the season's magenta fireweed. This is also when 60,000 beluga congregate to feed on Hudson Bay's capelin and Arctic char. It's possible to see these charismatic chalk-white whales by boat, Zodiac, kayak or even by AquaGliding, which involves donning a wetsuit and being pulled through the water on a floating mat. Some operators use hydrophones, so you can hear the underwater songs of these 'canaries of the sea'.

EXPERIENCES

STORM THE FORT: Built on Hudson Bay in the 1730s, Prince of Wales Fort is now a National Historic Site; tours are available July–August.

SAIL TO FIREWEED ISLAND: A summer trip to this outcrop in the bay may deliver both bear and beluga sightings, plus birds and wildflowers.

WALK WITH BEARS: Specialist operators run tundra hikes with expert guides, for the spine-tingling chance to spot polar bears on foot; hikes are best done in summer months.

GET A STAMP: Pop into Churchill's post office to receive a polar-bear stamp in your passport.

NEED TO KNOW

Churchill is a two-hour flight from Winnipeg, the capital of Manitoba. It is possible to make the journey by rail instead: a thrice-weekly, 1697km (1054-mile) two-day, two-night, Wi-Fi-free ride. Economy passengers travel on recliner seats; Sleeper Plus is more comfortable, with beds and access to a shower. Food is available on board; there is also a glass-roofed observation car.

Left, from top: Arctic terns in Churchill; polar bear near Churchill **Opposite:** Fireweed, Hudson Bay coast

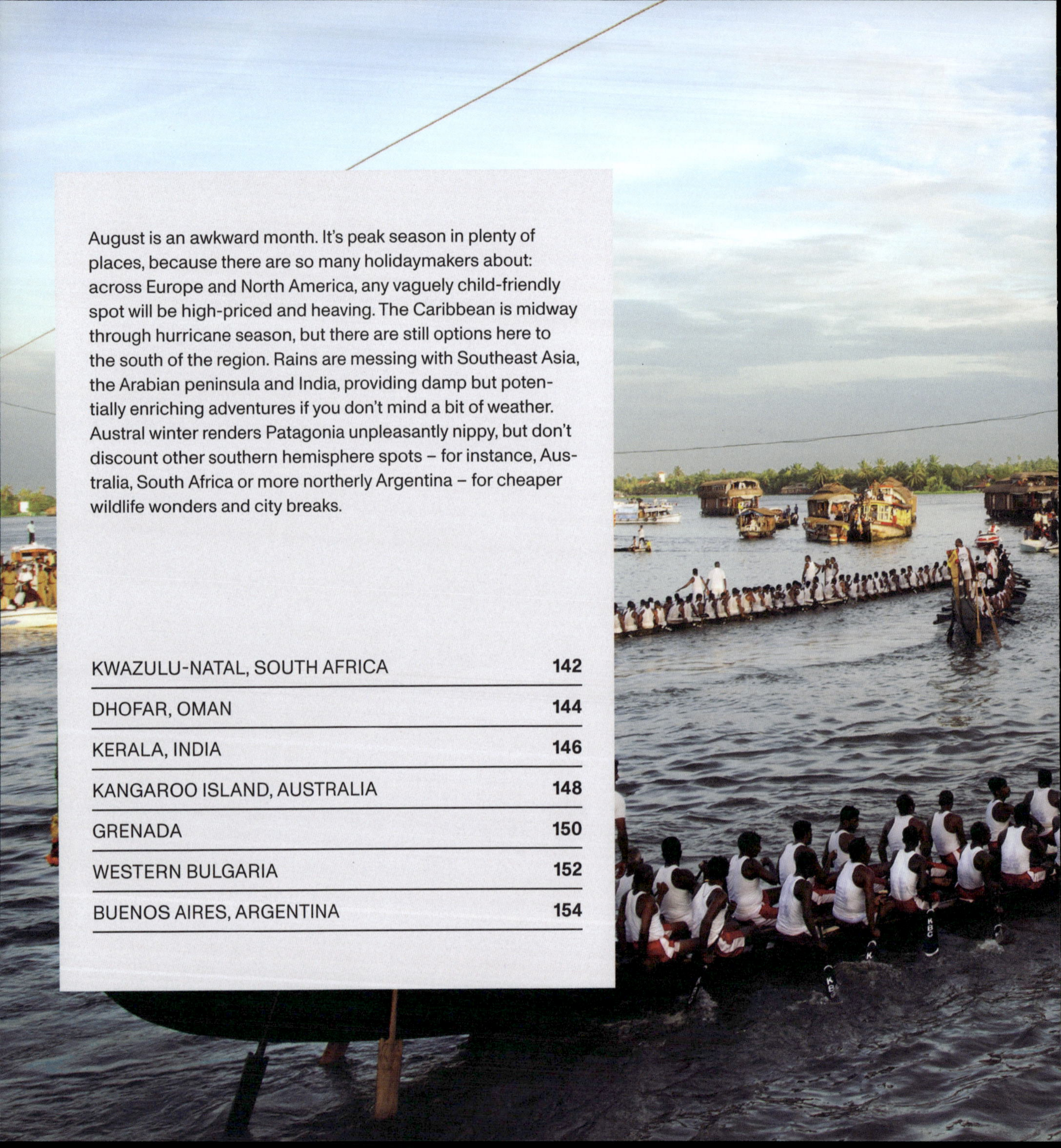

August is an awkward month. It's peak season in plenty of places, because there are so many holidaymakers about: across Europe and North America, any vaguely child-friendly spot will be high-priced and heaving. The Caribbean is midway through hurricane season, but there are still options here to the south of the region. Rains are messing with Southeast Asia, the Arabian peninsula and India, providing damp but potentially enriching adventures if you don't mind a bit of weather. Austral winter renders Patagonia unpleasantly nippy, but don't discount other southern hemisphere spots – for instance, Australia, South Africa or more northerly Argentina – for cheaper wildlife wonders and city breaks.

AUGUST

JUNE–AUGUST

WILD WINTER WONDERS

KwaZulu-Natal, South Africa

● Hooked on scorching sun, sea and sand? Maybe winter in this temptingly diverse province isn't for you. Come back December to February, when temperatures (but also rainfall and crowds) on Durban's beaches soar. But if tracking the Big Five and admiring marine mammals, plus roaming historic sites, discovering traditional Zulu customs and hiking some of the planet's most dramatically photogenic mountains is your thing, aim for August.

Exhibit A: Hluhluwe–iMfolozi Park – reputedly Africa's oldest wildlife reserve, declared in the 19th century – is dry and mild, with temps topping out around 25°C (77°F). With vegetation now sparse and wildlife gathering at shrinking water sources, it's prime time for spotting lions, buffalo, and white and black rhinos.

Exhibit B: the Battlefields Region, studded with poignant memorials and other reminders of the clashes between Zulus, Boers and British troops that defined the history of South Africa during the 19th century.

Exhibit C: cetaceans – the humpback and southern right whales that migrate along this coast between mid-May and November are easily seen from the shore, but a whale-watching boat trip gets you up-close and personal.

Exhibit D: the Drakensberg mountains, chilly at night but with clear skies and camera-friendly vistas by day – ideal for ambling.

EXPERIENCES

EXPLORE ISIMANGALISO WETLAND PARK: Cruise among hippos and mesmerising birdlife on Lake St Lucia; spot elephants, lions and buffalo on a safari drive; and take a whale-watching boat trip.

HIKE THE MOUNTAINS: Tackle relatively gentle Drakensberg trails like Tugela Gorge, or take a testing trek up Cathedral Peak.

BEHOLD HISTORIC BATTLEFIELDS: Join a guided tour or drive between the sites of key clashes: Anglo-Zulu confrontations at Isandlwana and Rorke's Drift; Anglo-Boer battles at Ladysmith and Colenso.

WALK WITH THE ANIMALS: Join an expert-led Wilderness Trails walking safari through Hluhluwe-iMfolozi Park.

NEED TO KNOW

Getting around KwaZulu-Natal is most convenient on a guided tour or as a self-drive adventure. Fortunately, roads are largely in good condition and, outside large towns, mostly quiet (be aware that speed bumps have spread like a rash in many areas). Car hire is easy and cost-effective, too – pick up wheels from Durban Airport and head north or east.

Left, from top: Hippo, iSimangaliso Wetland Park; Isandlwana memorials, Battlefields Region **Opposite:** Drakensberg mountains

Dhofar, Oman

JULY-SEPTEMBER

EMBRACE THE MONSOON

● Visiting Oman in high summer might seem crazy – but hear us out. Sure, the sweltering heat across much of the country at this time can feel debilitating, with highs heading up and over 40°C (104°F) in the north and among the desert dunes. It's far too hot to do much cultural exploring, but if you want to just flop by the pool or loll in air-conditioned luxe, there are cheap hotel deals to be found.

But southern Oman is a whole other thing. From late June to mid-September, the Khareef (monsoon) sweeps from the Indian Ocean onto the coconut-palm beaches of the Dhofar region. Trapped by the coastal mountains, it douses this otherwise arid expanse in light rains and cooling mists: oases bloom, waterfalls gush, fruit trees hang heavy, hills and valleys glow green.

While you're unlikely to see many foreign tourists, it's a dream ticket as far as Omanis are concerned. The three-month Khareef Festival (aka Salalah Tourism Festival) draws in thousands with musical performances, dagger-dance competitions, sports events, craft fairs, meat grills, frankincense-toting market stalls and general celebrations of the country's cultural diversity. Busy, perhaps – hotels bump up prices a bit – but offering fascinating insights into an alternative Oman.

Left: Ayn Khor waterfall, Salalah **Opposite:** Green turtle, Ras Al Jinz

EXPERIENCES

EXPLORE SALALAH: Dhofar's colourful capital is the hub of monsoon cultural activity. Visit the ruins of 12th-century trading port Zafar at the UNESCO-listed Al Baleed Archaeological Park.

WATCH TURTLES: Brave the heat of more northerly Ras Al Jinz in July or August for a chance to see both nesting mothers and new hatchlings on the beach.

FIND FRUIT: Stroll Salalah's banana, coconut-palm and papaya plantations and drink juice fresh from the trees.

GO GREEN: Make the most of the lushness on 4WD trips and hikes into the valleys; Wadi Darbat's waterfalls are especially photogenic.

NEED TO KNOW

Flights between capital Muscat and Salalah take under two hours. It's safest to explore the Dhofar region in a 4WD with an experienced driver–guide – rains can cause sudden and extreme flooding in valleys and dry riverbeds. Pack for wet, warm weather; women should also bring clothes that cover legs and arms, plus a headscarf to wear for mosque visits.

Kerala, India

AUGUST–SEPTEMBER

WELLNESS AND WATERFALLS

● South India during the monsoon – are you mad? Well, maybe, but there's method, right?

True, chances are it'll rain every day in August, if not all day. It's humid, and it's hot, with average highs of 29°C (84°F) on the coast. And the biting insects are out in force.

But – and there are several sizeable buts – the crowds are gone and the bargains are here. By August, downpours are easing – typically, less rain falls now than in June or July. Yet vegetation lining the famed backwaters and cloaking the hills is lusher than ever, burgeoning in impossibly vivid and varied shades of green. Cascades surge in the highlands – like 91m-high (299ft) Palaruvi Falls, its Malayalam name translating as 'stream of milk' in a reflection of its distinctive hue.

Fruits are beautifully ripe: peaches, pomegranates and more. Snake boats or *chundan vallam*, some 30m (98ft) long, surge along the backwaters in electrifying races. Cultural events celebrate the festival of Onam, usually in late August or early September. And by tradition the monsoon is the best time to experience rejuvenating Ayurvedic therapy; pores are open, ready to absorb oils and other treatments.

You might not top up your suntan – but for a quieter, cheaper, greener and healthier Kerala holiday, August's a hot ticket.

EXPERIENCES

WALK TO WATERFALLS: Trek to epic cataracts that thunder most powerfully during the monsoon – Athirappilly Falls, Kerala's largest, is 65km (40 miles) east of Thrissur.

ENJOY AYURVEDIC TREATMENTS: Book at a specialist resort or centre for massages, application of herbal oils, face masks and more.

SOAK IN THE SEA: Cool off between showers in the balmy Indian Ocean; water temps average at around 27°C (81°F) now.

GET FESTIVE: Relish the harvest festival of Onam, savouring cultural events and multi-dish Onam Sadhya vegetarian feasts, traditionally served on a banana leaf.

NEED TO KNOW

The monsoon is peak mosquito season, when biters breed en masse in standing water. Though Kerala has a relatively low prevalence of malaria, dengue fever can be a concern. In any case, it pays to reduce your chances of being bitten: wear long sleeves and trousers, spray with insect repellent and sleep under a mosquito net. Consider taking malaria prophylactics, too.

Left, from top: Sadhya feast during Onam; Athirappilly Falls **Opposite:** Varkala Beach

JUNE–AUGUST

SLOW-SEASON SUSTAINABILITY

Kangaroo Island, Australia

● Ain't nature brilliant? Back in 2020, bushfires ravaged almost half of Kangaroo Island – aka Karta Pintingga, Australia's third-largest isle – devastating homes, habitats and wildlife. But just a few years on, the island is rebounding: tourism businesses have rebuilt better, flora is flourishing, fauna thriving.

The island is a dream to explore at any time, but there's extra value in choosing the winter low season, not least because you'll be lending support to a recovering destination during the leaner months. Also, you're guaranteed a great experience. June to August sees far fewer visitors, but plenty of animal action: joeys begin to emerge from their kangaroo mothers' pouches, winter lambs gambol in the fields, seals and sea lions haul out in search of sunshine, and southern right whales swim by.

Cooler days – expect temperatures of 8°–15°C (46°–59°F) – make it a fine season for bushwalking, too. Yes, it might be wet, but that means lush vegetation, deserted beaches, thrillingly wild waves, full rivers and thunderous waterfalls – it's the perfect time to tackle the 5km (3-mile) Waterfall Creek hike in Flinders Chase National Park. And, after a day's bracing adventure, you'll find plenty of places to cosy up by a roaring fire with a glass of toothsome Kangaroo Island red.

EXPERIENCES

TAKE A HIKE: The 66km (41-mile) Kangaroo Island Wilderness Trail is one of Australia's official Great Walks, and the ultimate way to explore Flinders Chase National Park.

GO WILDLIFE-WATCHING: From kangaroos to wallabies, koalas to echidnas, the island overspills with iconic species; a good guide will ensure the best encounters.

EAT SLOW: Have a good yarn with local producers at the fertile isle's many farm gates and cellar doors.

SPOT WHALES: Coastal lookouts such as Penneshaw and Cape Willoughby (the latter home to a 19th-century lighthouse) afford good onshore viewing; boat trips are also available.

NEED TO KNOW

Kangaroo Island is a 45-minute ferry ride from Cape Jervis, on South Australia's Fleurieu Peninsula. Alternatively, flights link Adelaide and the island's Kingscote Airport (30 minutes). Day trips are possible but it's best to spend five to seven days here. Bring over your car on the ferry or hire one locally. The island has several charging stations for electric vehicles.

Left, from top: Kangaroo Island vineyards; kangaroos **Opposite:** Remarkable Rocks, Flinders Chase National Park

Grenada

AUGUST

LOWER PRICES, BIGGER PARTIES

● August is low season on the 'Spice Isle'. But it's also when Grenada is spiciest – and we're not referring to its profusion of nutmeg and cloves. Most Caribbean islands go wild for Carnival earlier in the year, but Grenada's Spicemas culminates in the first few weeks of August, coinciding with the hotter, wetter weather and the middle of the hurricane season. Thankfully, the island lies at the southern edge of the region's hurricane belt, so it's hit far less often by damaging storms.

And a bit of rain never dampens local spirits. Spicemas is a celebration of enthusiastic exuberance, colourful costumes, banging soca music, raucous fetes and some singular traditions. Among these is J'ouvert, an early morning parade of horned-helmet-wearing Jab Jab masqueraders slathered in black oil (it gets messy).

That's the madness of early August – off-season for outsiders, not so for Grenadians, and a complete cultural eyeopener. Alternatively, come in late August for peace, quiet and lower prices. The turquoise seas are at their warmest (28°C/82°F) – lovely for swimming at idyllic beaches. Head for huge, headline-grabbing Grand Anse; pretty Duquesne (where there are also Amerindian petroglyphs); and secluded Levera (part of Levera National Park), where turtles nest April to August.

EXPERIENCES

EAT OIL DOWN: Grenada's national dish, oil down is a hearty stew of breadfruit, ground provisions, callaloo, meat, coconut milk and spices.

DIVE INTO ART: Molinière Underwater Sculpture Park comprises nearly 100 coral-encrusted pieces; snorkel and dive trips are possible.

EXPLORE INLAND: Trails snake among the forested ridges of Grand Etang National Park and lead to wonderful waterfalls, such as the multiple cascades of Seven Sisters.

RAISE A GLASS: Running on hydropower since 1785, River Antoine Estate is the oldest distillery in Grenada; take a tour to see how rum's made.

NEED TO KNOW

If you're planning to embrace Spicemas, book well in advance, from flights, hotels and costumes to tickets for the many fetes – all-inclusive parties that range from comfy-casual to high glamour. Main events are Carnival Sunday; J'ouvert and Monday Night Mas on Carnival Monday; and the Parade of the Bands (including Moko Jumbie stilt-walkers) on Tuesday.

Left, from top: Molinière Underwater Sculpture Park; Grand Anse **Opposite:** Spicemas, St George's

Western Bulgaria

JULY–AUGUST

MELLOW MOUNTAINS AND MONUMENTS

● Bulgaria's peaks and pistes grab the kudos (and crowds) for budget ski breaks – but in summer they're adventure playgrounds for hikers exploring remote trails and pinch-me-picturesque ridges. In fact, the very highest regions, thronged with skiers in winter, are accessible to hikers only in July and August. That's when capital Sofia and historical hub Plovdiv nudge 30°C (86°F), sending locals flocking to the Black Sea coast and leaving streets and sights clear for travellers.

Start in Sofia, a beguiling, buzzing mishmash of ancient history, Communist-era chic and hip cafe culture; escape the heat by ducking into a Roman basilica or Ottoman mosque, then head to the hills. Closest are the Rila Mountains, where the country's highest peak, 2925m (9596ft) Musala, promises an achievable challenge, and paths lace emerald ridges, valleys and the glacial Seven Rila Lakes. To the south, the alpine vistas of Pirin National Park draw peak-baggers to 2914m (9560ft) Vihren. Further east, closer to Plovdiv, curious rock formations beckon in the Rhodope Mountains; delve into the Devil's Throat Cave and traverse the sheer-sided limestone cleft of the Trigrad Gorge.

Plovdiv's a cultural hot-spot: catch an opera at the Roman amphitheatre; browse creative Kapana quarter; or cool off in the Contemporary Art Halls, housed in an Ottoman-era bathhouse.

EXPERIENCES

HEAD FOR HEIGHTS: Scale Bulgaria's loftiest peaks – Musala in the Rila Mountains and Vihren in Pirin National Park – while they're accessible in high summer.

SOAK IN CAFE CULTURE: Chill with the locals on the terraces of Vitosha Blvd in Sofia or Kapana in Plovdiv, sampling *palachinki* (pancakes) or 'princesses' (mincemeat and cheese toasties), plus great coffee.

MARVEL AT MURALS: Be dazzled by the vivid frescoes and distinctive candy-striped architecture of Rila Monastery.

SAVOUR STREET ART: Join a free guided tour to admire Sofia's eye-catching and ever-evolving graffiti scene.

NEED TO KNOW

Buses trundle to towns like Govedartsi (for the Rila Mountains, a little over two hours) and Bansko (Pirin National Park, around three hours) from Sofia, and Pamporovo (for the Rhodope Mountains, around two hours) from Plovdiv, but they're relatively infrequent. Banding together with other travellers to book a taxi delivers convenience and speed, for only a little more cash each.

Left, from top: Roman amphitheatre, Plovdiv; Rila Monastery **Opposite:** Central Plovdiv

JUNE–AUGUST

TANGO TIME

Buenos Aires, Argentina

● Even in the depths of the southern winter, when the mercury rarely climbs above 15°C (59°F), the *milongas* (dancehalls) of the Argentine capital sizzle. This is the birthplace of tango, a dance with moves so steamy it was banned in some US and European cities in the early 20th century. And when tourism cools off in Argentina, triggering deals on flights and rooms, the tango action heats up: top performers bring their A-game to Buenos Aires for the Festival de Tango each August. Catch a show, or try tango yourself with a lesson and maybe a freestyle late-night hop with expert locals, fuelled by the city's famous steaks – best enjoyed *asado* (barbecue-style) at a neighbourhood *parrilla* (grillhouse) – and fine red wines.

Save some spark for daytimes, though. This buzzing capital is jammed with vibrant and varied barrios: leafy, elegant Palermo and neighbouring Recoleta, with its stately museums and celebrity-packed cemetery. Or street-art-daubed, bohemian San Telmo and kaleidoscopic La Boca, its cobbled Caminito area lined with historic, higgledy-piggledy, multihued houses. La Boca is also the location of the sheer-sided stadium known as La Bombonera, home to Argentina's most successful football club, Boca Juniors – go all out to bag a ticket to a Superclásico derby match against local rivals River Plate.

EXPERIENCES

MAKE YOUR MOVES: Take in tango basics with a lesson in a neighbourhood *milonga*, then stick around for the late-night free-for-all dance-off.

ENCOUNTER EVITA: Roam Cementerio de la Recoleta's miniature city of the dead and pay your respects to local celebrities, including Eva Perón, whose resting place is usually festooned with flowers.

RAISE THE STEAKS: Settle in at one of the city's famed steakhouses, savouring succulent cuts from cattle raised on the pampa grasslands and char-grilled to perfection.

COLOUR ME CURIOUS: Explore the artsy boutiques, galleries and cafes of rainbow-hued La Boca district.

NEED TO KNOW

Buenos Aires is easy to get around by public transport, with a good subway system and extensive bus network – buy a SUBE card from a kiosk. It's also a mellow city for walking and cycling. Bag a country two-for-one by riding the ferry to Uruguay – it's just 75 minutes to the irresistibly picturesque city of Colonia del Sacramento, twice that to capital Montevideo.

Left, from top: Tango dancers; La Bombonera stadium **Opposite:** La Boca district

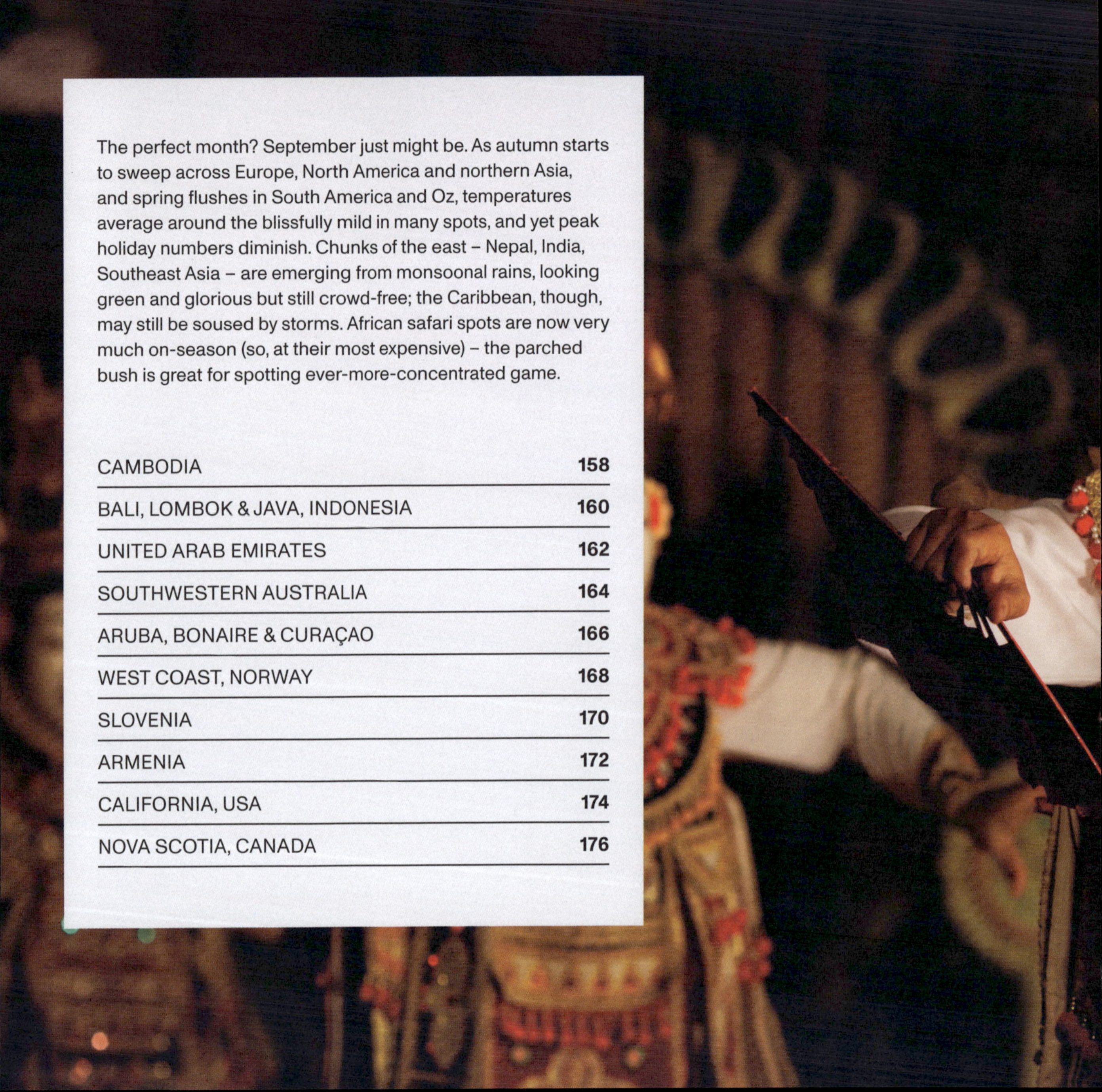

The perfect month? September just might be. As autumn starts to sweep across Europe, North America and northern Asia, and spring flushes in South America and Oz, temperatures average around the blissfully mild in many spots, and yet peak holiday numbers diminish. Chunks of the east – Nepal, India, Southeast Asia – are emerging from monsoonal rains, looking green and glorious but still crowd-free; the Caribbean, though, may still be soused by storms. African safari spots are now very much on-season (so, at their most expensive) – the parched bush is great for spotting ever-more-concentrated game.

SEPTEMBER

SEPTEMBER–OCTOBER

REFLECTED GLORIES

Cambodia

● Angkor's a fever dream. A sprawling complex of sandstone temples and tanks, ornately carved with enigmatic faces and episodes from ancient myths. A dizzying, dazzling vision, it's Buddhist but also Hindu, extrovert but also secretive, parts still swathed in jungle. And it's never more mesmerising than in the cool, pellucid air following a 'green season' downpour, with the mind-melting mini-mountains reflected in full moats and pools.

What Angkor's not full of in September is tourists. They thronged its temple precincts and walled Angkor Thom city from November to March, but started dripping away from April when temperatures began to soar, evaporating further when the rains came in earnest from May. By the end of summer, though the monsoon's still in full swing, downpours last only an hour or two – damping down the heat as well as crowds and prices.

There are extra bonuses: at the September equinox you can witness the spectacle of the sun rising directly over the central pinnacle of Angkor Wat; Buddhist temples explode with colour during Pchum Ben (Festival of the Dead) around this time. Elsewhere, Phnom Penh is packed with cultural highlights, the mighty lake of Tonlé Sap is full, rice paddies glisten, and wildlife and waterfalls are at their most alluring in nature reserves.

EXPERIENCES

MARVEL MORNING GLORIES: Admire the ancient, intricately carved temples of Angkor reflected in the brimming *barays* (reservoirs) and moats at sunrise.

CHILL IN THE CAPITAL: Visit Phnom Penh's Silver Pagoda and Royal Palace, then cool off with cocktails on Bassac Lane.

FLOAT YOUR BOAT: Take a tour to experience daily life among the floating villages on Tonlé Sap, near Siem Reap.

COOL OFF UNDER CASCADES: Admire the surging waterfalls of Bokor National Park and paddle through the 'Green Cathedral' near Kampot before browsing the town's night market.

NEED TO KNOW

Travel in remote rural areas, particularly Cambodia's wild east – Ratanakiri and Mondulkiri – can be challenging after heavy rains. Angkor tickets are available for durations of one (US$37 at the time of writing), three (US$62) and seven (US$72) days. The various monuments are spread over a wide area, so allow plenty of time – it's best to spring for a longer pass.

Left, from top: Phnom Kulen waterfall; Angkor Thom **Opposite:** Ta Prohm temple

Bali, Lombok & Java, Indonesia

SEPTEMBER–OCTOBER

SHOULDER-SEASON SWEET SPOT

● Picture a tropical paradise: golden sands, shoreline temples, snorkelling and smiles. Bali, right? Well, yes – but newsflash: you're not the only one to peg Indonesia's volcanic gem as your island of dreams. Those beaches get rammed in July, August and Christmas holiday times. And tropics mean monsoons – November to March is soggy season.

But sneak in between the midyear peak and later downpours (visitor numbers drop off during September and rains start to ramp up in October), and you'll find lower rates, emptier attractions and mostly sunny days in which to explore temples and cultural delights in Ubud, roam extraordinary rice terraces at Jatiluwih and Pupuan, or ride surf breaks off western beaches.

Bali overshadows its neighbouring islands, but both Java and Lombok are awesome, too. Head west to be wowed by two mighty monuments near Yogyakarta: the Hindu complex of Prambanan, and Borobudur – the world's largest Buddhist temple – stopping off to climb to the rim of Gunung Bromo's smouldering crater. To the east, don mask and snorkel to experience the best of Lombok's Gili Islands, swim off seductive Pantai Mawun beach, or conquer 3726m-high (12,224ft) Gunung Rinjani, the country's second-highest volcano.

Left: Ubud rice terraces, Bali **Opposite:** Pura Taman Saraswati, Ubud

EXPERIENCES

JOIN THE CULTURE CLUB: Drink in the arts and ambience of Ubud's galleries, museums and Hindu temples, enjoying a stroll through the so-called Monkey Forest inhabited by Balinese macaques.

SNORKEL THE REEFS: Be dazzled by tropical fish and come nose-to-snout with inquisitive turtles off Gili Meno.

RIDE THE WAVES: In September and October, west-coast surf breaks around Uluwatu, Padang Padang and Suluban offer options for all levels.

CLIMB A VOLCANO: Gunung Bromo (Java) is an easy-ish ascent with spectacular views from the crater rim; Rinjani (Lombok) is more challenging but also rewarding.

NEED TO KNOW

It's getting hotter and rainier from September through October, though downpours are usually short and sharp – find a beach bar or temple to shelter in till the drips stop. Flights link Denpasar on Bali with Yogyakarta and Surabaya on Java, and with Lombok; for Gili Trawangan, catching a ferry might be more convenient and pleasant.

United Arab Emirates

SEPTEMBER–OCTOBER

HIGH TEMPS, LOW PRICES

● Autumn is unconventional across the UAE. Palm trees don't turn golden colours, and in September the mercury is still pushing 35°C (95°F). But it is cooling from the inferno that is July and August, making it possible – especially as the season rolls on – to visit comfortably, taking advantage of hotel bargains and quieter sites.

One boon of the hot daytime temperatures is that nights stay warmer, too – all the better to enjoy stargazing excursions into the desert. Stellar spots include Abu Dhabi's Al Sadeem Astronomy, which runs guided tours and night-sky observation sessions; and Dubai's Al Qudra Lakes, in the Al Marmoom Desert Conservation Reserve, where there's minimal light pollution. Or stay at a desert safari camp in Ras Al Khaimah to sleep under the stars.

To beat the heat during the day, seek out watery attractions. Traditional waterparks such as Wild Wadi are packed with flume-filled fun; wilder Al Ain Adventure offers surfing and white-water kayaking. Alternatively, retreat to air-conditioning. Wander inside the cool, cultured walls of the Louvre Abu Dhabi, a striking museum charting the history of art from the Neolithic to the 21st century. Or head for the Mall of the Emirates, where Ski Dubai provides year-round skiing and snowboarding.

EXPERIENCES

DO A DUNE BASH: One of the UAE's biggest thrills is a 4WD ride into the desert; head out early to avoid the worst of the heat.

SEEK GREENERY: Abu Dhabi's Al Ain Oasis is shaded by 147,000 date palms and still has its original falaj irrigation system.

TRAVEL THROUGH TIME: Dubai's architecturally spectacular Museum of the Future challenges visitors to imagine what the world might be like in 2071.

APPRECIATE THE ANCIENT: Artefacts dating back 125,000 years have been found at Sharjah's Mleiha archaeological site; excursions into the Mars-like landscape can include overnight camps.

NEED TO KNOW

Public transport between the seven emirates that make up the UAE is limited. Useful air-conditioned bus routes include Dubai to Abu Dhabi (1½ hours), Abu Dhabi to Al Ain (around 2½ hours) and Dubai to Ras Al Khaimah via Sharjah (around 1½ hours). Taxis are the easiest way to make shorter journeys; Dubai has a two-line Metro that connects the main sites.

Left, from top: Wild Wadi Waterpark, Dubai; driving in the dunes, Rub al Khali Desert, Abu Dhabi **Opposite:** Campsite in Ras al Khaimah

Southwestern Australia

SEPTEMBER–OCTOBER

SOUTHERN SPRING

● It's b(l)oom time in the west – the pivot point when the seasons recognised by Indigenous Noongar people flip from Djilba (August–September, the months of wild-flowers) to Kambarang (October–November, welcoming warmth and birth). The tail-end of the winter rains have watered 8000-plus flowering species that explode into bloom across the region: banksias, vanilla lilies, fairy orchids and rare mountain villarsia. Drier times are here again, but come now and you'll sneak in before the school break and the arrival of summer crowds on beaches and reserves.

There are more botanical marvels to admire here, too. Head to Pemberton and into Gloucester National Park, where you can scale one of the world's loftiest tree species, the karri, which can grow up to 90m (295ft) high. Or get up close and personal with the vast red tingle trees of Walpole-Nornalup National Park, clambering up to the Tree Top Walk to wander among the burliest eucalypts in the Valley of the Giants.

Surf's up (and bottoms up) in WA's wine capital, Margaret River, where surging spring swells boost surf adventures. You won't be the only one making a splash: humpback whales are performing marine gymnastics off the southern coast as they migrate between June and October.

EXPERIENCES

TAKE A HIKE: Tackle a section of the epic Bibbulmun Track, stretching 1003km (623 miles) from Perth to Albany, or stroll the 123km (76-mile) trail between Cape Naturaliste and Cape Leeuwin.

WINE AND DINE: Tour Margaret River's vineyards, pairing choice drops with fine local cheeses and chocolate.

ENCOUNTER PLAYFUL LEVIATHANS: Admire the acrobatic breaches and fin-slapping antics of humpback whales on a guided cruise from Albany.

SCALE A GIANT: Stroll the Tree Top Walk among huge tingle trees in Walpole-Nornalup National Park, or climb a colossal karri in Gloucester National Park.

NEED TO KNOW

Buses operated by Transwa and South West Coachlines serve the coast from Perth down to Augusta; there's a handy train from Perth to Bunbury, too. You can also fly from Perth to Albany in just over an hour. Public transport is patchy in the rest of the region, though – self-drive's the easiest way to explore.

Left, from top: Vasse Felix winery, Margaret River; wildflowers near Morawa **Opposite:** Tree Top Walk, Walpole-Nornalup National Park

AUGUST–OCTOBER

LOW SEASON, STORM-FREE

Aruba, Bonaire & Curaçao

● The dreamy ABCs, afloat in the southern Caribbean, are unlike the region's other isles. Formerly part of the Netherlands Antilles, they're a hair's breadth from the Venezuelan coast and – importantly for off-season sunseekers – sit south of the hurricane belt. This means they're not prone to the extreme weather that renders much of the Caribbean riskier at this time of year. So, while you might get a little more rain here now than in the December–April peak season, in general the weather is still pretty idyllic.

And despite their mellow climate, they attract far fewer visitors than their neighbours, so you'll find your paradise break is a whole lot cheaper. But which island to choose? If you want beach after drop-dead-gorgeous beach plus the liveliest nightlife of the three, US-influenced Aruba is for you.

If you prefer a more laid-back vibe, coupled with world-beating scuba diving and snorkelling, opt for Bonaire: it's encircled by a National Marine Park, and many of the 85 dive sites are accessible direct from the shore.

If you want a good dose of culture with your Caribbean bliss, head for Curaçao, the largest of the ABCs. It's here you'll find the most galleries and museums, plus the colourful capital, Willemstad, bedecked with Dutch-era architecture.

Left, from top: A Bonaire iguana; Oranjestad, Aruba **Opposite:** Diving, Bonaire National Marine Park

EXPERIENCES

LEARN THE HISTORY: Sited within a 19th-century merchant's house, Museum Kurá Hulanda tells the story of the enslaved people transported to Curaçao.

HIT THE WAVES: Aruba and Bonaire offer epic kitesurfing and windsurfing; conditions are excellent at this time.

PICK A BEACH: There are lots of lovelies, including Aruba's wide, sandy Eagle Beach and Curaçao's tiny Playa Piskadó, great for snorkelling with turtles.

REVEL IN NATURE: Bonaire's Washington Slagbaai National Park is a craggy enclave of cliffs, caves, coast, trails, snorkel spots, iguanas and flamingos; hike up Brandaris, the island's highest point.

NEED TO KNOW

Spawning – when corals release their eggs and sperm en masse into the water – occurs only a few times a year. Around the ABCs this usually happens between August and October, always at night, during a full moon. Night dives can be organised to witness the spectacle. The Caribbean Research and Management of Biodiversity station releases annual reports predicting when it might occur.

West Coast, Norway

SEPTEMBER–OCTOBER

CRUISING WITH AUTUMN COLOURS

● On an autumn voyage along Norway's fjord-nicked, mountain-flanked west coast, you might get *all* the seasons in one trip. The classic journey covers 2500 nautical miles, from southerly Bergen to Kirkenes and back again. Setting off in September/October means an increasing intensity of flaming autumn colours as you surge north into the Arctic Circle, up to landscapes already snow-dusted and wintry.

Ships run year-round on this unique voyage – part adventurous tourist cruise, part vital ferry and cargo boat serving Norway's coastal communities. There are 34 ports of call, and plenty of spectacular sites en route; as a bonus, autumn voyages make detours into Trollfjord and Hjørundfjord, two of the country's most superbly scenic waterways.

Another plus: cabins are cheaper now than in high summer, when warmer temperatures and midnight sun attract the most travellers. However, there's still plenty of daylight for sightseeing: more than 15 hours a day in Tromsø during September, still 11 hours in October (polar nights start drawing in from November). And, thanks to generally clearer weather, autumn is an excellent time to glimpse the aurora – from October to March, cruises come with a northern lights guarantee, so if you don't see dancing lights in the skies, you get another voyage for free.

Left: Northern lights, Tromsø Opposite: Arctic Cathedral, Tromsø

EXPERIENCES

EAT THE SEASON: The ships' galleys focus on local produce, and autumn is peak harvest time; expect fresh seafood, foraged mushrooms and handpicked cloudberries.

STRETCH YOUR LEGS: Walk through the hole in the legendary granite dome of Torghatten; amble the coast in Bodø; or hike around Hjørundfjord and the Sunnmøre Alps.

EXPLORE THE CITIES: Stops include beautiful Bergen, Art Nouveau Ålesund, historic Trondheim and Arctic capital Tromsø – don't miss a candlelit concert inside the latter's cathedral.

LEARN WHILE YOU SAIL: Onboard lectures cover topics ranging from Sámi culture to the northern lights.

NEED TO KNOW

Hurtigruten has been sailing the Norwegian coast since 1893. Its vessels are comfortable but not luxurious. Rival operator Havila launched plusher, low-emission ships on the same route in 2021. Both aim to be zero-emission by 2030. The full Bergen–Kirkenes–Bergen round-trip takes 12 days, but shorter options are possible. All food and tea/coffee is included on board; alcohol and optional excursions cost extra.

Slovenia

SEPTEMBER–OCTOBER

LATE SEASON, STILL SUPERB

● Ah, Slovenia. This compact and charming nation ticks so many boxes, yet somehow manages not to be as overrun with visitors as its better-known neighbours. Its chocolate-box-cute capital, Ljubljana, isn't as touristy as Budapest. Its short but sweet Adriatic coastline isn't as crowded as Croatia. Its thrilling hiking and biking trails amid the majestic Julian Alps aren't as busy as those in Austria. Its historic and increasingly highly rated vineyards are far less visited than those in Italy. Even in high season, Slovenia is a good choice.

Save your visit until autumn, though, and things get better still. September sees the crowds thin – hot-spots such as fairy-tale Lake Bled will be even more enjoyable. Plus temperatures mellow nicely, with ideal weather for treks in Triglav National Park, tackling alpine mountain-bike trails and long-distance rides, or rafting and canyoning on the emerald-green Soča River.

And, as the country is almost 60% covered in trees, you can also expect some superb autumn shows: top spots include the hidden Logar Valley; the larch-lined Vršič Pass; and the vine-striped hills of the Podravje region, where you can toast the harvest with a glass of local Furmint. If the weather turns chilly? Warm up in one of Slovenia's natural thermal spas.

EXPERIENCES

TACKLE TRIGLAV: Slovenia's 2864m-high (9396ft) mountain is a national icon; it's best climbed August to September, when snow is rare and storms less frequent.

LINGER BY THE LAKES: The mountain-fringed waters of Bled and Bohinj are even more gorgeous when gilded with autumn colours.

GO WINE TASTING: The grape harvest is underway in September – join an organised harvest visit to lend a hand, or simply sip at a cellar door.

HEAD UNDERGROUND: Shelter from autumn rain in gargantuan Karst-region caves Postojna and Škocjan; they stay a cool 12°C (54°F) year-round.

NEED TO KNOW

Slovenia was the first country declared a Green Destination of the World. Its suggested code of conduct for visitors includes using businesses that have been awarded the Slovenia Green Label; travelling by public transport, bike or on foot; sticking to paths to avoid damaging nature; conserving water and energy; eating local produce; and respecting locals and their culture.

Left, from top: Ljubljanica river, Ljubljana; Primorska region wine and charcuterie **Opposite:** Lake Bled

Armenia

SEPTEMBER–OCTOBER

COOL AUTUMN

● Ain't nowhere quite like Armenia in autumn. Squeezed between Türkiye, Georgia, Azerbaijan and Iran, Armenia shares similarities with neighbouring nations in its architecture, art, cuisine and culture. Yet, as the proud local people will proclaim, this compact, mountainous, landlocked land came first. Noah's great-grandson settled here, according to legend, and capital Yerevan was founded in 782 BCE, making it older than Rome.

What'll you find here? History and tradition galore, of course. Ancient monasteries perched above sheer river-carved gorges, plus prehistoric petroglyphs, troglodyte homes and one of the planet's earliest astronomical observatories, Karahunj, a megalithic circle dubbed 'Armenia's Stonehenge'. But also a smorgasbord of flavours: flaky *borek*, lavash flatbread, lamb kofta and rice pilaf, dried fruits and stuffed vine leaves. Season-ripe fruits range from luscious apricots (which reputedly originated here) to watermelons or persimmons. Booze, too: the oldest-known winemaking equipment was discovered here, and Winston Churchill loved a nip of Armenian brandy.

More importantly, autumn's ideal for exploring, now that sizzling summer temperatures – and crowds – have subsided. Hike pine-shaded trails that spider Dilijan National Park and the Tavush region in the mountainous northeast, and discover mesmerising churches and monasteries ringing with chants, their glorious frescoes lit by candles.

EXPERIENCES

FEAST ON FRESH FLAVOURS: Browse Yerevan's covered market to pick up apricots, watermelons, dried apples, cheeses and *basturma* (spiced dried beef).

RIDE HIGH TO HEAVEN: Ride the 5.7km-long (3.5-mile) Wings of Tatev cableway to its namesake 9th-century monastery, thrilling to vertiginous views.

LEARN TO MAKE LAVASH: Get hands-on with a baking lesson, making Armenia's famed (and delicious) flatbread in a distinctive barrel-shaped oven.

TAKE TO THE TRAILS: Hike the forested 'Little Switzerland' mountains of Dilijan National Park, cooling off in shady pools.

NEED TO KNOW

It's pretty easy to bolt on a visit to Armenia's northerly neighbour, Georgia – reputedly the birthplace of wine, and a spectacular place for hiking the Caucasus Mountains and discovering the country's unique culture. You could DIY – direct buses between Yerevan and Georgian capital Tbilisi take just over five hours – but a guided tour will get you to more remote and fascinating spots.

Left, from top: Armenian *ghapama* (stuffed pumpkin); Tatev Monastery **Opposite:** Byurakan Astrophysical Observatory

SEPTEMBER–NOVEMBER

RIPE FOR ROAD-TRIPPING

California, USA

● Raring for a road trip? Cool California beckons now: golden days, crashing waves, epic landscapes, far fewer people. The Pacific Coast Hwy between LA and San Francisco is pure magic. Monterey County – roughly midway – even calls this the 'secret season' for its sunshine, sea breezes and temperatures around a delicious 25°C (77°F). Even better, accommodation prices dip after Labor Day (early September) and don't rise again until Thanksgiving (late November).

Begin in San Francisco, where summer fog lifts to reveal bright, balmy days, then head south, winding past Big Sur's rugged cliffs and stopping to look out for whales, sea otters and dolphins. Did we mention that September is California Wine Month? Harvest festivals are held everywhere, from Napa to Paso Robles; with a designated driver behind the wheel, you can swill and sip your way through autumn, visiting the state's 6200-odd wineries without the crowds.

If you steer inland, you'll find California's national parks stripped of summer visitors. Yosemite is still warm enough for a camping trip, its great grey rocks and evergreens speckled with flashes of autumn colour. Further south, Joshua Tree's searing heat is easing, allowing comfortable hikes amid its surreal boulder formations and namesake plants, as well as stargazing beneath some of California's clearest night skies.

Left, from top: Twin Lakes, Mammoth; Hidden Valley Campground, Joshua Tree National Park **Opposite:** Bixby Bridge, Big Sur

EXPERIENCES

DRIVE TIOGA RD: Hit the only road traversing the whole of Yosemite; it's generally closed by snow from late October.

LEAF-PEEP: California's fall colours burst mid-September to November; for early autumnal displays, drive through the aspen groves of Sonora Pass or via the lakes of Mono County.

MAKE TIME FOR TAHOE: Enjoy all the lake's summer activities in warm September sunshine, just without the crowds.

GO BOULDER: There are more than 6000 climbing routes in Joshua Tree National Park; mild-but-warm autumn days are great for clambering over the rocks.

NEED TO KNOW

California is a whale-watching hot-spot, but sightings vary by season and location. Monterey Bay, on the Central Coast, is one of the very best places to see them. Blue whales are most commonly spotted here May to October, humpbacks March to November, orca late August to October. You might also encounter sea otters, California fur seals, elephant seals and numerous types of porpoise and dolphin.

Nova Scotia, Canada

SEPTEMBER–OCTOBER

AFTER THE SUMMER SCRUM

● As far as most tourists are concerned, high summer is high time to be in Nova Scotia. It's when the sun shines brightest, and every hiking trail, hotel room, patio, theatre show and sea-salty site is open for business. But ask a Nova Scotian? They'll say autumn is best. Yes, temperatures start to drop, but so do numbers of both bugs and visitors.

This is a foodie province, and September to October is one of the best times to feast. Farmers' markets brim with locally-grown fruit and veg; menus feature seasonal specials such as hodgepodge stew and blueberry grunt. It's also ideal for hitting the Good Cheer Trail, Canada's first winery, brewery, cidery, distillery and meadery route. You'll find the grape and apple harvest underway, and producers happy to pour you a glass.

Fin, minke and humpback whales are still splashing around the Bay of Fundy in autumn, too; whale-watching trips run till mid-October. Fundy is also home to the world's biggest tides, a mind-bending phenomenon that's best understood on kayak trips or at gourmet dinners served at tables on the sandy seabed. And as the season progresses, Nova Scotia's forests become increasingly fiery – the Cape Breton Highlands National Park is a top leaf-peeping spot.

EXPERIENCES

DRIVE THE CABOT TRAIL: This world-class road trip loops Cape Breton, at its fiery best when trees are on the turn.

COSY UP: If the weather chills, pick one of the province's cute towns – Annapolis Royal, Lunenburg, Wolfville – and hunker down at an atmospheric old inn.

CATCH A TUNE: French Acadian and Gaelic Scottish music culture is alive and well in bars and dancehalls; the Celtic Colours International Festival is held in October.

HIT THE TRAILS: Routes around Cape Breton, around Fundy's Cape Chignecto and in Kejimkujik National Park are much quieter in autumn.

NEED TO KNOW

Nova Scotia's main airport is Halifax Stanfield International in the capital. VIA Rail's Ocean service links Halifax with Montréal (23 hours). A high-speed ferry links Bar Harbor (Maine, USA) and Yarmouth, Nova Scotia (3½ hours) from mid-May to mid-October. There are also ferry services between Nova Scotia and New Brunswick (year-round), Newfoundland (year-round) and Prince Edward Island (May–December).

Left, from top: Bay of Fundy; blueberry grunt **Opposite:** Cape Breton's Cabot Trail

Outstanding October is up there with September for discerning off-season travellers. Its mists and mellow fruitfulness provide pleasantly cool, quiet, atmospheric and foodie-central conditions across many northern destinations, from Canada to the Greek isles – visit now before tourist-focused businesses shut for winter. Asia is variously cooling down (as in Mongolia) or drying up (Southeast Asia), but tourist crowds have yet to descend – the exception being in the Himalaya: this is peak trekking time. There's also refreshing spring fun to be found across plenty of South America, and places like Peru aren't wet yet. However, Central America remains at its soggiest.

OCTOBER

Tunisia

OCTOBER–NOVEMBER

FILMIC FALL

● Tunisia may be North Africa's smallest nation, but don't be fooled – this compact cracker stretching from the Sahara to the Mediterranean has a technicolour cinematic soul. Countless moviemakers have revelled in its stellar locations: the cast of Monty Python's *Life of Brian* were Very Naughty Boys in Monastir; Indiana Jones whip-cracked in Kairouan for *Raiders of the Lost Ark*; and Luke Skywalker escaped dusty Tatooine – or, Matmata – in *Star Wars*, to name just a few.

In high summer, despite simmering at around 35°C (95°F), Tunisia's beaches stage their own crowd scenes, with casts of thousands thronging the sands. By autumn, though, mercury and masses are waning – time to shoot your own reels at epic sites like the monumental Roman colosseum of El Jem, which provided a lookbook for *Gladiator*, or the Roman amphitheatre at Dougga. Alternatively, lose yourself amid the gorgeous white-and-blue villas of clifftop Sidi Bou Saïd, or in the medieval medinas of Tunis and Sousse, studded with magnificent mosques, palaces and fortifications.

This is a fruitful time to head south, too: olives are ripening in the groves around Sfax, while plump dates are plucked from palms around the oasis towns of Kebili and Tozeur; and the latter is another destination that's hosted Jedi, Indy – and Ralph Fiennes in *The English Patient*.

EXPERIENCES

SINK INTO THE SAND: Sun-soak on the beaches of Hammamet or Djerba Island, where Muslim, Amazigh and Jewish communities have coexisted for centuries.

TAKE A ROMAN HOLIDAY: Explore astonishing Carthage, founded in the 9th century BCE but rebuilt by the Romans with baths, theatres, villas and exquisite mosaics.

FIND A COOL MEDINA: Delve into the warren of alleys in Kairouan's walled quarter, seeking out the 9th-century Great Mosque.

SEE SIDI BOU SAÏD: Visit galleries and palaces in this gorgeously gleaming coastal town, beloved of artist Paul Klee and poet Edith Sitwell.

NEED TO KNOW

You can, of course, fly to Tunisia from major cities worldwide – but arriving by boat is much more romantic. Ferries sail to Tunis from Palermo (Sicily), Marseille, Genoa, Salerno and Civitavecchia, near Rome. English isn't widely spoken in Tunisia, particularly outside beach resorts; practise your French or, ideally, Arabic.

Left, from top: Sidi Bou Saïd shops; Gulf of Tunis from Sidi Bou Saïd **Opposite:** Mausoleum of Habib Bourguiba, Monastir

Seychelles

OCTOBER–NOVEMBER

AWESOME UNDERWATER

● When you say 'Seychelles' you might just as well say 'paradise'. This Indian Ocean archipelago, lazing a smidgen south of the equator, epitomises that word: a scattering of 100-plus isles fashioned from the whitest sand, the smoothest boulders, the frilliest palms and the turquoise-est seas. The weather is always tropical (temperatures are consistently 24°–32°C/75°–90°F), with fluctuations in heat, wind, rain and humidity at the ocean's whim – only semi-predictable, and varying by location.

The peak (and priciest) season is the cooler June–August period, but wait until October and you're in for a treat. This month marks the transition between brisker southeasterly trade winds swapping to lighter northwesterlies. The result? Particularly calm weather that creates perfect snorkelling and diving conditions, with epic visibility revealing everything from vibrant reefs and shipwrecks to turtles, stingrays, clownfish and moray eels. Plus, whale sharks are often seen September to November.

Where to start? Use local ferries to combine the mountainous main island of Mahé with laid-back, car-free La Digue and knockout Praslin. Elsewhere, Bird Island is, unsurprisingly, brilliant for birds – October to November is ideal for spotting many migrant species. Harder-to-reach Outer Islands, such as Desroches, Alphonse and Astove, offer some of the best diving in the world.

EXPERIENCES

SEE TURTLES: Nesting season for hawksbills runs October–December; unusually, females here lay during the day – see them at the reserve on Cousine.

JOIN THE PARTY: Festival Kreol, the Seychelles' biggest cultural event, is held across Mahé in late October.

ADMIRE NATURE: Praslin's Vallée de Mai is the world's smallest natural UNESCO site; it's here that you'll find the endemic coco de mer palm, with its suggestive-looking seeds.

GO WILD: The far-flung Aldabra Group, 1150km (715 miles) from Mahé, is the Galápagos of the Indian Ocean, home to 150,000 giant tortoises.

NEED TO KNOW

From May to September, prevailing trade winds can cause large amounts of seaweed to wash up on the southeast- and south-coast beaches of the main islands. From October to April, as the wind shifts, seaweed is more likely to hit the northwest coasts. It isn't dangerous, but can blight otherwise perfect-looking beaches. Many hotels run free shuttle buses to unaffected bays.

Left, from top: La Passe, La Digue; Madagascar fody, Bird Island **Opposite:** Anse Source d'Argent, La Digue

OCTOBER–NOVEMBER

NORTH-SOUTH DIVIDE

Vietnam

● In this long, legendarily diverse country, the weather's all over the place – literally. When the sun smiles on central beaches around Nha Trang and Hội An, rain lashes Hanoi and the north. And when skies clear over Huế, downpours drench the sandy strands of Phú Quốc and the Côn Đảo islands. Sure, you're pretty safe everywhere in February or March – so long as you don't mind crowds. That's Peak Season, capital P; in fact, visitor numbers are high everywhere December to April, and again July to August as sunseekers descend on the coast.

There's a precious (geographically split) window in autumn, though, when tourist numbers and prices slump just as the weather's picking up in the north and south. Paths dry out for treks through the Hoàng Liên Sơn Mountains or between Hmong villages around highland hub Sapa. The karst outcrops of Hạ Long Bay start to gleam again beneath clearer skies, and Hanoi's Hoàn Kiếm Lake glistens in the sunshine.

Bunny-hop over the central region, sodden by storms, to cruise the waterways of the Mekong Delta and feel the hype of Ho Chi Minh City (Saigon) – and if the heavens open, head into the warren-like Cu Chi Tunnels to immerse in Viet Cong history.

Left, from top: Vietnamese *phở* (noodle soup); Fansipan, Hoàng Liên Son Mountains **Opposite:** Mekong Delta

EXPERIENCES

HAVE HIGH TIMES: Take to the trails to discover indigenous Hmong culture in villages around Sapa, or conquer Vietnam's loftiest summit, 3143m (10,312ft) Fansipan.

CARVE OUT CAPITAL IDEAS: Explore Hanoi's enchanting Old Quarter, visiting temples, museums and parks, and slurping *phở* (noodle soup) on street corners.

TAKE CRUISE CONTROL: Board a junk to sail between the otherworldly limestone pinnacles, islands and grottos of Hạ Long Bay.

ENJOY DELTA VIEWS: Base yourself in Ho Chi Minh City to roam the villages and floating markets of the Mekong Delta, laden with freshly harvested produce.

NEED TO KNOW

While both northern and southern Vietnam are heading into dry seasons, storms still lash the central region. Heading to Huế's historic Imperial City and Hội An's charming Old Town? Pack your umbrella, not your swimsuit – beach weather this ain't. The north tends to dry up earlier than the south, so ideally start your jaunt in Hanoi and end at Ho Chi Minh City.

Mongolia

SEPTEMBER–OCTOBER

WHEN FEATHERS FLY

● If you absolutely, positively have to get away from it – or them – all, aim for the world's most sparsely populated country, home to just 2.2 people per square kilometre (about 1% of the population density of Malawi or Nepal) in an area three times the size of France. Yet even in Mongolia there are moments when you might feel a bit squeezed. Specifically, summer: the vast majority of visitors arrive between June and August to explore the Altai Mountains, delve into the arid expanses of the Gobi Desert and experience nomadic life-styles on the endless steppe. Numbers (and, as it happens, rains and mosquitoes) peak in mid-July when Mongolians compete in the 'three manly sports' of wrestling, horse-racing and archery at the Naadam Festival in capital Ulaanbaatar.

As autumn takes hold, crowds, costs and temperatures crank down. This is a fine and drier time to discover Mongolia's fascinating culture and wild, empty landscapes, with steppe and slopes verdant and photogenic. Expect sunny days and chilly nights – pack thermals to cope with subzero evenings under felt in traditional *gers* (yurts), ducking below -10°C (14°F) around lovely Lake Khövsgöl. To warm you up, cheer to the spectacle of regal raptors performing aerial feats during eagle festivals in Sagsai (September) or Bayan-Ölgii (October).

Left: Kazakh eagle hunters, Bayan-Ölgii **Opposite:** Gandan Khiid, Ulaanbaatar

EXPERIENCES

TAKE STEPPES: Roam Mongolia's endless grasslands, riding steeds among wild horses in Khustain National Park or Bactrian camels in the dunes of 'mini Gobi', Elsen-Tasarkhai.

GO NOMAD: Taste timeless lifestyles with a night or two in a *ger* homestay, maybe learning to make traditional Mongolian dumplings.

ENJOY JUST DESERTS: Venture into the Gobi Desert to admire the flaming-red sandstone cliffs of Bayanzag and the sheer-sided Yolyn Am canyon.

EYE EAGLES: Watch Kazakh hunters display their skills with trained birds of prey at the Bayan-Ölgii Golden Eagle Festival.

NEED TO KNOW

If you do visit an eagle festival, bear in mind that the birds are used to their handlers but not so many other people – be sensitive and avoid crowding these incredible creatures. Vegetarians beware: most Mongolian food contains mutton in one form or another. It can also seem bland to outsider tastes – consider bringing a condiment or two to add zing.

Cyclades, Greece

OCTOBER

EMPTIER ISLES, BALMY SEAS

● Come summer, when temperatures blaze, it can seem the whole world has descended on the 33 inhabited islands that make up this gorgeous archipelago in the Aegean. Holiday-makers simply can't resist the Cyclades' splendid beaches, cute white-blue paint jobs and ineffable, adorable Greekness.

And damn, it's busy. Overloved islands such as Santorini and Mykonos are more bunfight than chill-out, and you definitely need to book ferry tickets in advance. Opt for October instead and you'll hit a sweet spot: that moment before many businesses shut up shop for the winter, but after most tourists have gone home. The sea is still blissfully warm, temperatures still top 20°C (68°F), and you simply have more space.

It's far more comfortable for exploring too, making autumn a good time to delve into the Cyclades' rich human history. You might explore Syros, a fascinating mix of Venetian Catholic and Orthodox Greek influences, with fine buildings to admire. The entire island of Delos, where Apollo was reputedly born, is a UNESCO-listed archaeological site. Then there's untouristy Andros, where the volunteer Andros Routes organisation maintains around 240km (150 miles) of hiking paths, created as a means of preserving ancient ways and enabling visitors to discover the island's culture on foot.

EXPERIENCES

WALK ALL ANDROS: The flagship hike is a continuous 100km (62-mile) trail, crisscrossing the island between coast and mountains, north to south.

VISIT VOLCANIC ISLES: Enjoy dreamy, caldera-clinging Santorini without the summer crowds, or opt for lovely, lower-key alternatives like Milos.

EXPLORE ERMOUPOLI: Lively year-round, the Cycladic capital, on Syros, is full of fine churches and handsome mansions.

SEEK OUT SIFNOS: This quiet Cycladic isle is like the Greece of yore: traditional villages, uncrowded beaches, walking trails and simple tavernas; look out for local speciality *revithia* (chickpea stew).

NEED TO KNOW

Ferries to the Cyclades depart frequently from Piraeus and Rafina ports, near Athens. A full schedule runs June–September; tickets (available online) should be booked well in advance during this period, especially for popular routes. In April–May and October–November, ferries run less frequently, but most routes still offer multiple services daily. A reduced timetable runs December–March.

Left, from top: Hiking on Andros; a church in Ermoupolis, Syros island **Opposite:** Andros

Menorca, Spain

OCTOBER

MILD ISLAND TIMES

● Ibiza might be shutting down – the Closing Party season on the clubber's isle runs mid-September to mid-October – but there's still plenty of joy to be found on Menorca, its mellower Balearic sister. The whole island is a designated UNESCO Biosphere Reserve, and the still-warm days of autumn are ideal for discovering why, without the crowds. Sure, you might be sprinkled by the odd shower, but skies are bright, seas are balmy, and the temperature just right for roaming around.

And roam around you should. Right around. The 185km (115-mile) Camí de Cavalls coastal trail was first dreamed up in the 14th century to enable knights to patrol the shores, defending the island from would-be invaders. Now it's a terrific hike, horseback ride or (tough) mountain-bike adventure that takes in every cliff, cove and beach.

Too much effort? How about some twitching at the bird-busy wetlands of Parc Natural S'Albufera des Grau – you might spot Egyptian vultures, osprey and booted eagles. Or admiring four-millennia-old megalithic monuments at mazelike Ciutadella. Or kicking back in handsome capital Maó (Mahón), blessed with Anglo-Spanish heritage and, in October, the annual Cheese Fair – try a chunk of bold, buttery Maó, or head to a *quesería* (cheesemaking dairy) for a tour.

EXPERIENCES

GET ARTY: The hip Hauser & Wirth Menorca gallery, on formerly abandoned Isla del Rey, hosts changing exhibitions; it's open May to late October, and is accessible by ferry.

TAKE A DIP: Swim in still-warm (around 23°C/74°F) waters at beaches such as rose-gold Cala Pregonda, powder-white Cala Mitjana or low-key Cala Macarelleta.

CHURN CHEESE: Subaida Farm, which makes Mahón-Menorca DOP artisan cheese, runs 'Farmer Family For a Day' tours; have a go at making your own.

TREK EL TORO: Enjoy panoramic views from Menorca's highest point, which tops out at 358m (1175ft).

NEED TO KNOW

Menorca's airport is just outside Mahón. Regular year-round ferries link the island to Mallorca (one hour), Barcelona (four to eight hours) and Valencia (16 hours). Menorca has a good network of more than 40 bus lines, which link most towns and villages, and numerous resorts; airport and round-island services run year-round; many beach services are summer-only.

Left, from top: Maó cheese; Cala Macarelleta **Opposite:** Osprey with prey

OCTOBER–NOVEMBER

SUN, SAND, SPRING

Rio & the Coast, Brazil

● Rio, baby! Brazil's pin-up city has it all: the sweeps of sand at Leblon, Ipanema and, of course, Copacabana; Sugarloaf Mountain (396m/1300ft) soaring above Guanabara Bay; and Maracana Stadium. In summer, add samba and swarms of visitors thronging the city and surrounding beaches: between December and March, wall-to-wall parties pack the streets – most thrillingly during Carnaval, when floats and dancers wow the Sambadrome.

Get in early, as the heat (and, gradually, rain) begins to build in spring, and you'll enjoy this spectacular region's full attention without hordes of rival visitors. And not just Rio. To the east lies Búzios, just a sleeping fishing hamlet till Brigitte Bardot put it on the map in the 1960s – but even today, the beaches speckling the peninsula are mostly serene in spring. Head west to trace the scalloped shoreline of the Costa Verde, flanked by the lush emerald canopy of the Atlantic Forest and bookended by the beautifully preserved Portuguese architecture of Paraty.

And offshore floats another gem: Ilha Grande, long off-limits as a pirate's redoubt then a penal colony, today a car-free paradise where hikers roam the rainforest and sun-worshippers lounge on more than 100 beaches.

EXPERIENCES

POOTLE AROUND PARATY: Amble the cobblestoned Old Town, admiring gleaming 18th- and 19th-century buildings and savouring fresh seafood.

GET BEACHY IN BÚZIOS: Recline on one of 17 strands fringing the peninsula, maybe rousing yourself to surf or snorkel.

FIND YOUR RHYTHM: Take the pulse of Rio at a sizzling Lapa district samba club, or toast the Cidade Maravilhosa (Marvellous City) with a sunset caipirinha cocktail overlooking Ipanema.

ESCAPE TO ISLA GRANDE: Book into a traditional *pousada* (guesthouse) in Vila do Abraão, then stride out to explore the rainforest or swim from golden sands.

NEED TO KNOW

In this tropical paradise you can expect rain some of the time – and fortunately Rio, in particular, has ample indoor attractions, including fine museums and art galleries. As a bonus, many offer free entry on one day a week – check the latest details online – or, like the eye-wateringly beautiful Real Gabinete Português de Leitura (Portuguese Reading Room), are always gratis.

Left, from top: Samba club, Rio's Lapa district; Sugarloaf Mountain cable car, Rio **Opposite:** Paraty Old Town

Okanagan Valley, Canada

OCTOBER

MELLOW FRUITFULNESS

● There's a golden glow about Canada's greatest grape-growing region this month. From Osoyoos, on the US border, to Vernon, 180km (112 miles) north up this British Columbia valley, the landscape is starting to transform from lush-green and fruit-heavy to shades of yellow and red. Autumn is taking hold of the Okanagan – and it looks magnificent.

This is one of Canada's warmest, sunniest regions, and though temperatures are dropping now, so too are the crowds, meaning more space at cellar bars for tastings, and better deals on cute cottages tucked amid the vines. Plus in October, the markets are brimful of local produce, and farm-to-fork restaurants serve seasonal goodies.

You could drive Hwy 97, which connects Osoyoos (surrounded by Canada's only true desert, best explored at this cooler time of year) with Vernon. This route runs via Oliver (host of the Festival of the Grape every September/October), Okanagan Falls, the lively town of Penticton and outdoorsy Kelowna (a great place for a hike), passing countless vineyards en route. Alternatively, explore on two wheels. The Kettle Valley and Okanagan Rail Trails, both developed from abandoned train tracks, provide excellent paths to pedal via the region's lakes, hills and vines.

Left: Vineyards by Vaseux Lake, Okanagan Valley **Opposite:** Hiking Vernon

EXPERIENCES

SIP FIRST NATIONS WINE: Indigenous owned-and-operated Nk'Mip Cellars, overlooking Osoyoos, creates award-winning wines; on-site tastings are available.

HIKE VERNON: Tucked amid hills and surrounded by three lakes, Vernon is known as the 'Trails Capital of BC', with 50 routes to choose from.

DRINK BEER: Okanagan isn't all about wine – Penticton is big on craft beer too; follow its Ale Trail to hop between breweries.

SEE AUTUMN COLOURS: The deciduous trees along the Mission Creek Greenway bike-and-hike trail network near Kelowna add fiery colour to Scenic Canyon.

NEED TO KNOW

The Similkameen Valley, just west of the Okanagan, is a lesser-known alternative. It receives more hours of sunshine, nurturing different grape varieties, and some of BC's best fruit is grown here. It's also Canada's organic farming capital, with a wealth of farmers' markets and roadside food stalls. The villages of Keremeos and Cawston are good hubs for visiting artisan wineries.

Isle of Skye, Scotland

OCTOBER–NOVEMBER

NO MASSES, NO MIDGES

● Oh, splendid yet stressed Skye! This lauded Hebridean Isle is cursed by its own rugged good looks. In high summer season, the peaks, peninsulas, bays, lochs, roads and hotel rooms of Scotland's second-most-touristed spot (after Edinburgh) are overrun with people. So wait it out and visit in late autumn. It's just as gorgeous but the masses (and the midges) have fled, and the prices have fallen. Plus the night skies are spectacular – with luck, the northern lights might put on a show; there's especially good viewing on the remote, light-pollution-free Waternish Peninsula.

Many businesses reduce their hours or shut up shop as winter approaches, but there's still plenty to do. For instance, golden eagles, sea eagles, otters and seals don't go anywhere; the resident red deer will be rutting, too. And you can still explore the island's must-see landscapes – such as the Cuillin Hills, magical Fairy Glen and the wild rock formations of the Trotternish Peninsula – with far fewer other people.

The weather can be variable, although that's true year-round – they don't call Skye the 'Cloud Isle' for nothing. But if the rain, cold and haar (coastal fog) really set in, use it as an excuse to warm up with a dram from one the island's whisky distilleries.

EXPERIENCES

SAIL TO RAASAY: The ferry from Skye to this wee isle runs year-round; walk to ruined Brochel Castle and raise a glass at Raasay Distillery.

SPOT WILDLIFE: A dusk hike through spectacular Glen Sligachan offers a good chance of spying red deer; shy otters are more likely to be seen in quieter months.

WALK TO THE QUIRAING: This basalt escarpment of cliffs and pinnacles is Skye at its most striking.

SURVEY THE SOUND OF SLEAT: Take a brilliant, bracing walk to the Point of Sleat Lighthouse, keeping eyes peeled for whales and dolphins.

NEED TO KNOW

Skye can be reached by road bridge from the mainland village of Kyle of Lochalsh, which has a train station; buses also run from the mainland. Ferries sail from Mallaig to Armadale (southern Skye) and from Tarbert, on the Isle of Harris, to Uig on Skye's Trotternish Peninsula. Local buses run across Skye, but services aren't frequent.

Left, from top: Red deer stag; whisky tasting, Isle of Skye **Opposite:** Old Man of Storr, Trotternish Peninsula

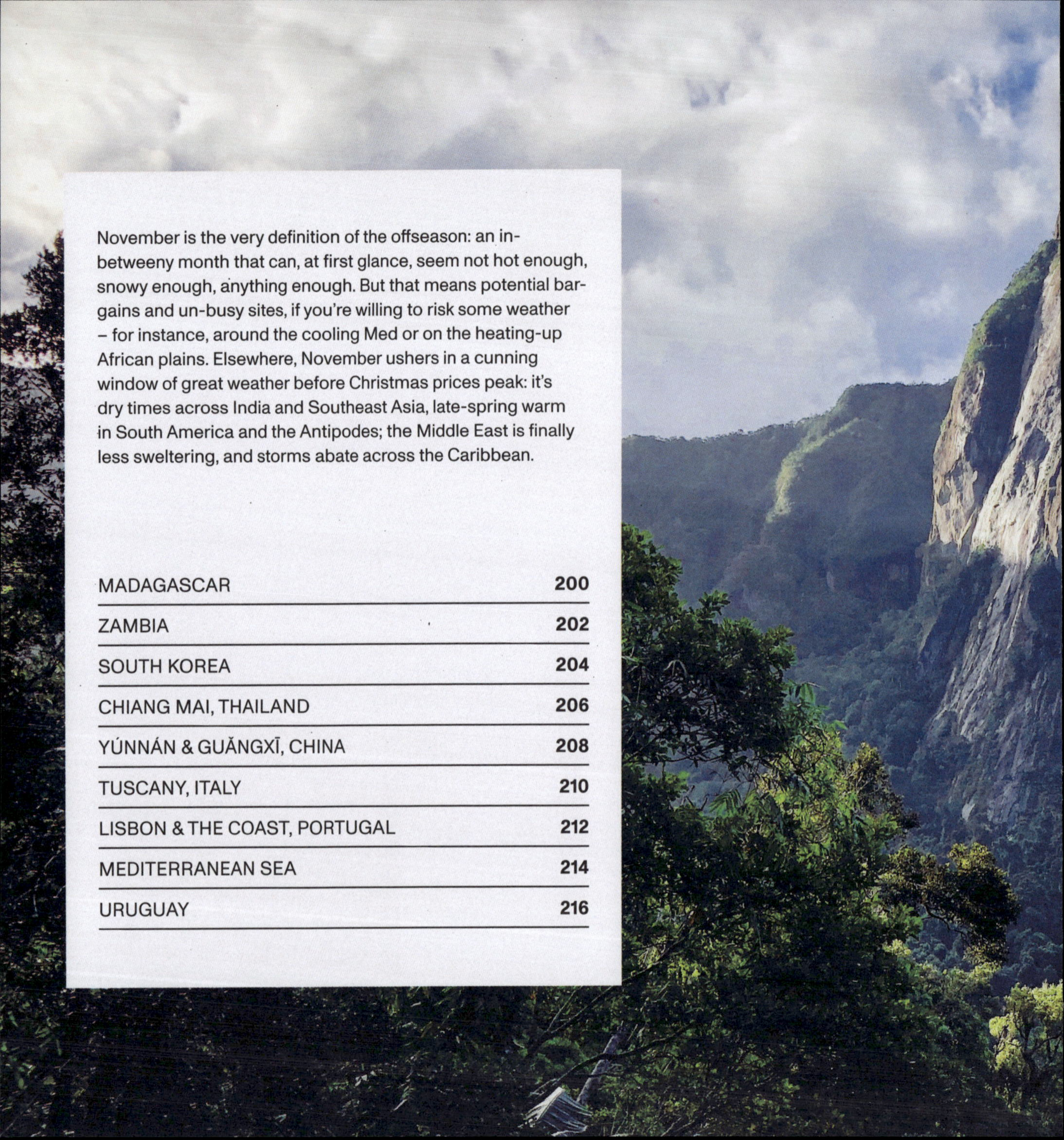

November is the very definition of the offseason: an in-betweeny month that can, at first glance, seem not hot enough, snowy enough, anything enough. But that means potential bargains and un-busy sites, if you're willing to risk some weather – for instance, around the cooling Med or on the heating-up African plains. Elsewhere, November ushers in a cunning window of great weather before Christmas prices peak: it's dry times across India and Southeast Asia, late-spring warm in South America and the Antipodes; the Middle East is finally less sweltering, and storms abate across the Caribbean.

NOVEMBER

SEPTEMBER–NOVEMBER

WILDLIFE WITHOUT CROWDS

Madagascar

● Lemurs, lemurs and yet more lemurs? Aye-aye, cap'n! That spindly-fingered nocturnal weirdo, the aye-aye, is just one species of the ancient primates getting creative on the 'Great Red Island' right now. The elusive mongoose-cat curio known as the fossa is most active in October and November – look (and listen) out for their noisy mating behaviour, as each female hooks up with maybe 10 males among the branches. And it's boom time for many lemurs, which give birth late in the austral summer and into spring – enjoy the antics of baby ring-tails or dancing sifakas.

No such boom in tourists, though: the usual holiday rules apply here, with the northern summer and December peak times for visitors. Dodge those months and you can enjoy relative solitude as you explore Madagascar's varied forests (dry, spiny, cloud and rain), plus baobab avenues, coastline, plateaus and the distinctive, needlelike karst outcrops called *tsingy*. As the end of the year approaches, both heat (nudging 30°C/86°F) and rainfall start to climb – but it's not till late November that downpours really return to capital Antananarivo and the east coast. Plus, the sea's warming up – a bonus for snorkellers finning the coral reefs off Toliara or Nosy Be, and meeting green and hawksbill sea turtles among Nosy Sakatia's seagrass beds.

EXPERIENCES

DANCE WITH LEMURS: Enjoy the spectacle of dancing sifakas – agile and acrobatic lemurs – in Berenty Reserve or Andasibe-Mantadia and Isalo National Parks, also home to ring-tailed and indri lemurs and chameleons.

GET CULTURED: Discover Malagasy culture, with visits to villages or towns such as Ambositra and beachside Ifaty.

GO FACE-TO-FACE WITH FOSSA: Head to Kirindy Forest or Anjajavy Private Nature Reserve as these elusive carnivores get clamorously polyamorous.

SWIM WITH GIANTS: Snorkel alongside the world's biggest fish, 10m-long (33ft) whale sharks, which cruise the waters around Nosy Be between September and December.

NEED TO KNOW

The rains tend to pick up first on the east coast – if you plan to visit later in November, max your time in western areas. Everyday Malagasy life is governed by a number of traditions unfamiliar to foreign visitors, not least systems of *fady* (taboos). Take advice from local guides about how to behave at sensitive times and places.

Left, from top: Fossa, Kirindy Forest; tsingy, Parc National Bemaraha **Opposite:** Allée des Baobabs

Zambia

OCTOBER–NOVEMBER

POST-PEAK PARKS

● No shade on other African destinations, but if you absolutely, positively demand the prime safari experience, Zambia's tough to top. Guides here are walking wildlife encyclopedias. They have to be: this land – specifically, South Luangwa National Park – is the birthplace of the walking safari, bringing you up-close and personal with all creatures great and small.

Getting the GOAT costs, of course – no-one's pretending Zambia's cheap. But the budget-conscious hold their nerve till the very end of the dry season (late October into November), when increasing heat deters many visitors. Camps that book out June to September tend to empty and offer discounted rates – just when wildlife-watching is at its best, with undergrowth sparse, infants appearing and hunts often witnessed.

South Luangwa tops the wish list for animal encounters on foot – twin with neighbouring North Luangwa to tick off the Big Five (lion, leopard, buffalo, elephant and rhino), and to encounter African wild dogs. Lower Zambezi NP's another hot-spot for large mammals and birds, particularly if canoe safaris float your boat. Quieter still is vast Kafue NP, where cheetahs sprint after prey across the plains. And in Kasanka NP, Africa's largest mammal migration is underway as some 10 million straw-coloured fruit bats roost, emerging each dusk in a breathtaking display.

EXPERIENCES

WALK WITH THE ANIMALS: Take a walking safari with an expert guide and armed scout in South Luangwa National Park, spotting lions, giraffes, hippos and much more.

TRACK THE OTHER GREAT MIGRATION: Mingle with the vast herds of wildebeest that trundle from Angola to Liuwa Plain National Park, joining stately cranes and cheetahs.

GO BATTY: Watch massed millions of straw-coloured fruit bats take off from their branches in Kasanka National Park.

HEAD FOR A FALL: Perch in the Devil's Pool on the edge of Mosi-oa-Tunya ('The Smoke that Thunders', aka Victoria Falls).

NEED TO KNOW

Timing the arrival of the rains isn't an exact science, but ideally visit late October or the first half of November, before downpours reduce animals' reliance on waterholes, dispersing wildlife and making animal-viewing less rewarding. The downside: temperatures peak at around 34°C (93°F) – walking safaris are feasible only early morning and evening, and Victoria Falls is less thunderous.

Left, from top: Devil's Pool, Victoria Falls; grey crowned crane, Liuwa Plain NP **Opposite:** Lower Zambezi NP

South Korea

OCTOBER–NOVEMBER

WEATHER-BASED WIND-DOWN

● South Korea has four distinct seasons: a frigid winter; a lovely, blossom-y (but busy) spring; a hot, muggy summer – and a golden autumn, the pick of the bunch. October–November is less crowded than April–June; humidity has dropped but temperatures aren't yet bitter, and Mother Nature is putting on her most passionate autumn show, from the bright-yellow ginkgo trees in downtown Seoul to the fiery forests on the mountainsides. Indeed, it's a great time to head out on a leaf-peeping hike, perhaps in Seoraksan National Park.

It's also an ideal moment for a more contemplative break. Koreans have a saying: '*Gaeureun dokseoui gyejeorimnida*' (Fall is the best season for reading), because it's a period of cool and calm. Embrace this restful vibe on a stay in one of the country's Buddhist temples. It's a chance to wake, eat and worship with the monks; join them for sunrise chanting, plant-based meals and the traditional Da-Seon tea ceremony – mindfully brewing and drinking a warm cuppa is the perfect activity for a crisp autumn day.

November is also traditionally Kimjang season, when families gather to prepare large batches of kimchi to ferment and last through the winter. Seek out Seoul's Kimchi Festival, usually staged in early November.

Left: Maitreya Buddha, Beopju-sa **Opposite:** Gwangjang Market, Seoul

EXPERIENCES

HIKE JIRISAN: The three-day Jongju Course across Jirisan National Park is fabulous in autumn, when the maples blaze red.

GRAZE SEOUL: Gwangjang Market is a great place to try Korean street food; Noryangjin serves up the freshest fish; and Namdaemun Market, which dates from the 15th century, sells everything.

STAY AT A TEMPLE: UNESCO-listed Beopju-sa, in Songnisan National Park, has a dramatic setting; Golgul-sa, just outside historic Gyeongju, comprises caves hewn into Hamwolsan Mountain.

CLIMB NAEJANGSAN: This peak in Jeonbuk-do offers some of the best views of autumn foliage.

NEED TO KNOW

Autumn is a fruitful time for foodies. It's the season of three lauded seafoods: blue crab, jumbo prawns and the intensely savoury gizzard shad, usually grilled or served as sashimi. Also look for vitamin-packed persimmons, Korean pears, pine mushrooms and napa cabbage, a staple of kimchi. *Jeon* (savoury pancakes) are popular, too. Note: when eating in a restaurant, tipping is not expected.

NOVEMBER

GREAT WEATHER, PRE-PEAK

Chiang Mai, Thailand

● Thailand's wet season brings heavy downpours, and plenty of them – not ideal for exploring. But November marks the start of the dry months. Rainfall decreases – indeed, this is when Thais celebrate Loi Krathong, a festival marking the end of the monsoon – but visitor numbers, especially earlier in the month, are still down on the December to February peak.

It's an especially fine time for trekking and touring in the north, around the winsome city of Chiang Mai. Cool days, with average daytime temperatures of 17°C to 26°C (63°F to 79°F), and perhaps even light sweaters needed at night, are pleasant for getting out and about. That might mean strolling Chiang Mai's many markets and ancient temples, meeting the artisans of buzzing Chiang Rai, ambling through misty tea fields (and maybe learning how to pick and prepare the leaves), or even hiking in the shadow of 2565m (8415ft) Doi Inthanon, the country's highest peak.

The finest lookout, though, is Doi Luang Chiang Dao, a steep pinnacle that lords over its namesake bird-filled wildlife sanctuary. The trail to the peak is only open November to February, with a limited number of hikers permitted per day. The payoff is an exquisite view over tropical forest laced with clouds.

Left, from top: Tham Lot; Mein/Yao hill-tribe artisans **Opposite:** Wat Phra That Doi Suthep

EXPERIENCES

OBSERVE ELEPHANTS: Northern Thailand has several elephant 'sanctuaries', but do some research before visiting, and choose observation-only sites focused on animal welfare such as ChangChill, near Chiang Mai.

TREK TO HILL-TRIBE VILLAGES: Chiang Rai's Hilltribe Museum & Education Center is a good place to gen up before booking a hike to countryside communities.

CAVE-DWELL: Tham Lot, near Soppong, is one of Thailand's largest caves; explore by guided hike, wade and raft.

TEMPLE-TOUR: Of the 300-plus temples in and around Chiang Mai, most prominent is mountaintop Wat Phra That Doi Suthep; it offers good city views.

NEED TO KNOW

Chiang Mai is connected to Bangkok by plane (one hour), overnight train (around 14 hours) and bus (12 hours). *Rót daang* – red pickup trucks that operate as shared taxis – are the main way to get around Chiang Mai. There are also buses and tuk-tuks, though the old centre is walkable. Scooters can be hired for exploring the surrounding area. Boat trips run on the Mae Ping River.

Yúnnán & Guǎngxī, China

OCTOBER–NOVEMBER

THE BEAUTIFUL SOUTH

● Like the most sensational Chinese banquet, the twin southern belles of Yúnnán and Guǎngxī offer a smorgasbord of spectacles. Skyscraping karst pinnacles? Check. Gorgeous hillside rice terraces? Check. Ancient cities and hill-tribe villages? Tropical forests and mountain peaks? White-sand beaches and hilltop temples? Check, check, check.

What they don't have – at least as year's end approaches – is a crowd-control problem. The weeks after the long National Day holiday (tip: avoid) see Chinese people stick to home and international visitors largely stay away, too. Result: hotels and attractions are quiet, so haggling is increasingly fruitful. And though the mercury's dipping, so's rainfall – most oppressive in the middle months of the year – and you'll still enjoy 20°C-plus (68°F) days at lower levels; for example in Guìlín or Yángshuò, bases for exploring the karst-lined Li River.

You'll find quintessentially Chinese wonders in both provinces, so if time's limited you could explore only one. But there's bonus content in both. Guǎngxī has raft-riding cormorant fishers near Yángshuò, and white-sand beaches around Běihǎi. Yúnnán has the canals and cobbles of Lìjiāng and the Ming-dynasty walls of Dàlǐ, plus mountain hikes from Shangri-la (formerly Zhōngdiàn), and tropical vibes in the Xīshuāngbǎnnà region. Twice as tasty.

EXPERIENCES

TAKE TO THE TERRACES: Visit picture-perfect stepped rice terraces like Longji (the 'Dragon's Backbone') near Lóngshèng in Guǎngxī, or at Yuángyáng in Yúnnán.

SAMPLE SOUTHEAST ASIA: Meet the hill tribes and other ethnic communities of Xīshuāngbǎnnà, a kind of 'little Thailand' cradled alongside Laos and Myanmar.

TREK TIGER LEAPING GORGE: Hike beneath 3900m-high (12,795ft) peaks through one of the world's deepest canyons, alongside waterfalls feeding the roaring Jinsha River.

SAVOUR LOCAL FLAVOURS: A steaming, spicy, meaty soup, Kūnmíng's *guòqiáo mǐxiàn* (meaning 'crossing-the-bridge noodles') is a favourite on chilly evenings.

NEED TO KNOW

China's National Day, 1 October, is marked with parades, fireworks, concerts and 'Golden Week', a seven-plus-day public holiday when families travel en masse. Don't plan to get anywhere during the first 10 days of October. In November, the mountainous north of both provinces gets wintry in earnest; the later you come, the further south you should aim.

Left, from top: Lijiāng Old Town, Yúnnán; Black Dragon Pool Park, Lijiāng **Opposite:** Longji rice terraces, Guǎngxī

Tuscany, Italy

NOVEMBER

CROWD-FREE FOODIE SEASON

● Tuscany? You pays your money, you takes your choice. Would you prefer to see this apogee of dreamy Italian-ness soaked in sunshine but drowning in other people? Or are you willing to gamble a bit with the weather to experience those hilltop towns, world-class galleries and cypress-lined backroads without the crowds?

November is one of Tuscany's quietest months. And the weather isn't so very bad – you may get rain, but daytime highs of around 16°C (61°F) are still quite lovely for strolling alongside the Arno in Florence, or sipping espresso at pavement cafes in insanely beautiful Arezzo, San Gimignano and Siena. And it's much easier to bag coveted tables region-wide at this time.

November has other advantages, too – not least the produce. Chestnuts are in abundance, and the scent of them roasting wafts through the streets. White truffles reappear, and San Miniato holds a festival to the precious fungi over the last three weekends of the month. The hunting season for wild boar starts 1 November, so dishes such as *pappardelle al cinghiale* (pasta with wild boar sauce) pop up on menus. The olive harvest also begins – a fascinating time to visit the villages, catch old presses in action and taste the *olio nuovo* (new oil).

EXPERIENCES

ADMIRE ART: Queues for Florence's many treasures in the Galleria dell'Accademia, Uffizi and the Medici palaces are far shorter – ideal for grey days.

STAY AT AN AGRITOURISMO: Farmstays offer a chance to cosy up in the countryside and perhaps get hands-on with olive harvests and truffle hunts.

DRINK CHIANTI: Vineyards are still tinged with autumn colour, and cellars are open for tastings.

DON AN APRON: Dodge iffy weather by signing up for a cooking class, making hearty Tuscan specialities like *castagnaccio* (chestnut cake) or *ribollita* (a soup made with beans and leftover bread).

NEED TO KNOW

While Tuscany's larger towns remain open for business in low season, the region's coastal resorts and some of the smaller hilltop villages – such as Montefioralle, Monteriggioni and Pienza – turn very quiet. December and January, outside the peak Christmas period, are also good months for avoiding the crowds, with festive lights adding a sparkle that combats the colder, damper weather.

Left, from top: Uffizi, Florence; olive harvest, Arezzo **Opposite:** Ponte Vecchio and the Arno riverfront, Florence

OCTOBER–NOVEMBER

COOL CULTURE, CARVING WAVES

Lisbon & the Coast, Portugal

● Chestnuts roasting on an open fire...no, it's not Christmas yet – just smells like it, in Lisbon at least. The tantalising aroma of *castanhas assadas* wafting along the alleys of the ancient Alfama district is just one of the joys of exploring the Portuguese capital as autumn starts to segue into winter.

It's also one that you'll share largely with locals; as wetter, cooler days come, tourists go. That means minimal queues at the still-sensational sights – the monumental medieval Castelo de São Jorge (Castle of St George), giving 360-degree views from its ramparts; the hulking Sé de Lisboa (cathedral), built in 1150 on the foundations of a Moorish mosque; and fascinating museums showcasing puppets. And it means good deals and easy eats without the need to book ahead.

If you can tear yourself away from the city, there are plenty more delights to discover nearby, all blissfully crowd-free. There's the mind-boggling Manueline cloisters and ornately decorated church of the Mosteiro (monastery) dos Jerónimos in Bélem, and the fantasy castles and palaces of Sintra. And then there's the breaks around Cascais, where surf's up yet temperatures still cling close to 20°C (68°F) – if it's blown out, the windsurfing's pretty epic, too.

EXPERIENCES

STIR YOUR SOUL WITH FADO: Thrill to the yearning songs of Lisbon's gloriously mournful and moving folk music in a cosy bar.

SATE CUSTARD CRAVINGS: Munch irresistible *pastéis de nata* – flaky custard pastries – at Lisbon's beautiful azulejo-tiled Antiga Confeitaria de Belém.

FEEL REGAL IN SINTRA: Take your pick from ruined, crag-perched Castelo dos Mouros (Moorish Castle), icing-sugar-sweet Palácio Nacional da Sintra, or kaleidoscopic Disney-fantasy Palácio Nacional da Pena.

RIDE THE WAVES: Take a surfing lesson or catch the breaks at Praia do Guincho, Carcavelos or one of the other wave-bashed beaches around Cascais.

NEED TO KNOW

Lisbon's historic yellow trams are a hoot to ride, but be alert for pickpockets on the most touristy routes – particularly the 28, which trundles through the Alfama and other historic districts. Trains from Lisbon to the coast are cheap, quick and frequent – under 40 minutes to Estoril, Cascais or Sintra from central stations, with one-way fares below €3 and several departures each hour.

Left, from top: *Pastéis de nata*; Praia do Guincho, Cascais **Opposite:** Palácio Nacional da Pena, Sintra

Mediterranean Sea

NOVEMBER–FEBRUARY

QUIET CRUISING

● As late autumn starts to ebb into winter, many cruise ships that have been summer-sailing around the Mediterranean turn west and make for the Caribbean. But a few remain, offering passengers a different take on the sea: a 'quiet season' cruise. Classic ports of call – Dubrovnik, Barcelona, Genoa – are far less crowded. There's no hours-long queue to ride a Venetian gondola, no elbow-barging through the crowds for that essential shot of Pisa's Leaning Tower; in general, you can explore at a more relaxed pace, in a more 'local' atmosphere.

It will be cooler, too; far more pleasant for hiking up to the Acropolis or wandering shade-poor sites such as Pompeii. And there are bargains to be found, with cruise lines offering big discounts to fill boats.

There is, of course, the weather to consider. Conditions on land might be nippy and damp – but a cruise is for sightseeing, not beaches, so that shouldn't stop play. Warm up with a Turkish coffee in İstanbul's Grand Bazaar, or escape the weather in the Vatican Museums. Conditions at sea are unpredictable, and you'll likely experience a bit of chop – though rough seas can well up at any time throughout the year. Pack seasickness pills and enjoy the (cheap) ride.

Left: Rome's Colosseum, Italy Opposite: Dubrovnik's Fort St John, Croatia

EXPERIENCES

BROWSE THE STALLS: Local markets feel more local when not overrun with masses of passengers from multiple cruise ships; and some Christmas markets – like Seville's festive fair – kick off in mid- to late November.

TUCK INTO SEASONAL SPECIALITIES: Try Istrian truffles, fresh-squeezed Spanish orange juice and Greek *lahanodolmades* (stuffed cabbage balls).

ENJOY THE WELCOME: Shopkeepers and restaurateurs will be less harried and more keen for your custom.

HIT THE BIGGIES: Now is the time to share sites like Barcelona's Sagrada Família and Rome's Colosseum with relatively few tourists.

NEED TO KNOW

Research your ship's stability and facilities before booking. Consider vessels with saunas and heated pools, heated panoramic lounges, onboard cinemas, lecture programmes and libraries or reading rooms. Excursion options may be more limited due to seasonal closures or weather conditions; check what is possible and remain flexible. Certain sailings may be timed to coincide with off-season festivals, such as Venice Carnival.

Uruguay

NOVEMBER

SUN, SAND, STEAKS, SERENITY

● What d'you think you know about Uruguay? That cows outnumber people pretty much four to one, maybe, or that it's South America's second-smallest country, tucked between Brazil and Argentina? It also has sensational steaks, from cattle reared on the rolling pampa. It has fine wines and fascinating history – particularly the UNESCO-listed, cobbled Barrio Histórico (Old Town) of Colonia del Sacramento, founded by Portuguese colonists in 1680. Most of all, it has a disproportionate number of gorgeous golden-sand beaches speckling its 660km (410-mile) coastline. And in summer (December–February) locals crowd Uruguay's strands and other highlights.

It's so crazy easy to enjoy these charms in peace – just come a few weeks earlier. November may be a little cooler than high summer, but rain barely varies – unlike crowds and costs at those glorious beach resorts. Most famous is jet-set Punta del Este, so-called 'St-Tropez of South America', but there are plenty more. Sea temperatures hover around the high teens and sometimes over 20°C (68°F) in November – OK for swimming and plenty warm for surfing. And by arriving before the masses, you'll also coincide with the visit of southern right whales that cruise along the coast from July to November.

EXPERIENCES

PLAY GAUCHO: Saddle up to ride cowboy-style across the pampa during a stay at a typical *estancia* (cattle station).

SIP AND SAVOUR: Taste Uruguay's signature Tannat red wine during a tour of vineyards and bodegas around Carmelo.

DANCE TO THE DRUMS: Thrill to the rhythm of *candombe* drummers and sensual tango dancers at a *milonga* (dancehall) or dinner dance in Montevideo.

SOAK UP THE SUN: Head to the coast to hit the beach and feast on seafood in solitude at mellow La Barra, or upmarket, boho José Ignacio.

NEED TO KNOW

Comfortable buses run frequently along the coast from Montevideo, taking a little over two hours from the centre to Punta del Este, less from Carrasco International Airport. Heading inland, public transport is limited; self-drive's best for exploring. It's easy to tag on a visit to Buenos Aires in neighbouring Argentina – just 75 minutes from Colonia del Sacramento, twice that from Montevideo.

Left, from top: Barrio Histórico, Colonia del Sacramento; Uruguayan *gaucho (cowboy)* **Opposite:** Punta del Este

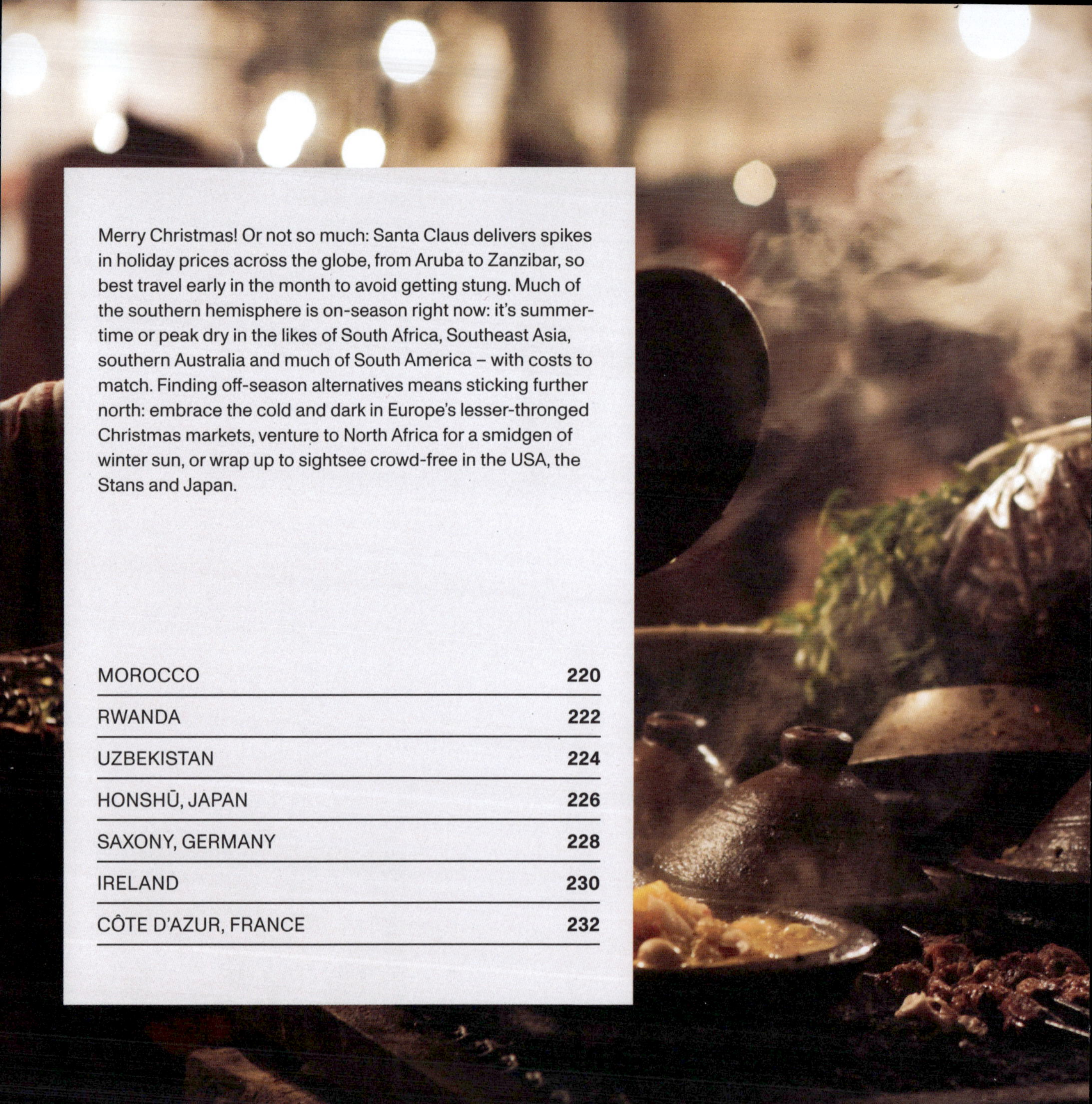

Merry Christmas! Or not so much: Santa Claus delivers spikes in holiday prices across the globe, from Aruba to Zanzibar, so best travel early in the month to avoid getting stung. Much of the southern hemisphere is on-season right now: it's summertime or peak dry in the likes of South Africa, Southeast Asia, southern Australia and much of South America – with costs to match. Finding off-season alternatives means sticking further north: embrace the cold and dark in Europe's lesser-thronged Christmas markets, venture to North Africa for a smidgen of winter sun, or wrap up to sightsee crowd-free in the USA, the Stans and Japan.

DECEMBER

DECEMBER–FEBRUARY

FUNKY COLD MEDINAS

Morocco

● Nowhere channels *One Thousand and One Nights* vibes quite like the historic walled hearts of Morocco's imperial cities. Aromas of spices, mint tea and tanneries waft through the medieval medinas of Fez and Marrakesh; their narrow, tangled alleys and souks (bazaars) pretty much unchanged since the 13th and 14th centuries. Winter's the time to wander in relative peace, exploring tucked-away palaces, admiring intricate tilework and carved decorations at ancient *medersas* (Islamic colleges), and tucking into hearty tagines and chickpea-laced harira soup as the street performers and hawkers of Marrakesh's Djemaa El Fna square warm up for the evening's mayhem. The International Film Festival draws cinephiles to Marrakesh each December, too.

This is also an ideal time to explore southern Morocco's varied landscapes outside the wilting heat of summer and busier, pricier spring and autumn. Seeking surf? Swells top out in winter, chasing across the north Atlantic to break at spots around Taghazout and Essaouira. Dreaming of deserts? Cool days and clear nights make Sahara stays a dream, riding camels through the dunes and gazing up at the constellations sparkling across the clearest skies. Pushing for peak practise? The High Atlas mountains are spectacular at any time, but an expert-guided snowy ascent of North Africa's loftiest summit, Toubkal, is something special.

EXPERIENCES

GET LOST: Delve into the labyrinthine souks and alleys of the ancient medinas in Fez or Marrakesh to discover medieval mosques and *medersas*.

TAKE A SUMMIT MEETING: Join a guided trek through the snow to the High Atlas peak of 4167m (13,671ft) Toubkal.

SPOT SHOOTING STARS: Gaze into the night sky above the Sahara to admire the sparkling streaks of the Geminids, the strongest annual meteor shower, peaking mid-December.

MAKE FOR A BREAK: Swells surge across the Atlantic throughout the winter months, creating dramatic surf breaks along Morocco's coastline.

NEED TO KNOW

Nighttime temperatures can drop to just a few degrees above freezing, especially in the Sahara and High Atlas, and many riads (traditional hotels) have minimal heating – bring warm clothes. December is one of Morocco's rainiest months; it's wettest in the north, much less so in Marrakesh, where prices rise as visitors arrive in numbers towards the end of December and into January.

Left, from top: Surfing, Taghazout; Souk Haddadine, Marrakesh. **Opposite:** Sahara Desert camp

Rwanda

DECEMBER

HIGH AND DRY(ER)

● Anywhere else, the allure of Volcanoes National Park would surely be geological, not zoological. In Rwanda, though, there's one big – very big – natural draw: the mountain gorilla. Indisputably the greatest ape, silverbacks can grow to 180kg (400lb) and stand 1.7m (5.6ft) tall – and trekking up to 3000m (9843ft) altitude to encounter such a huge patriarch guarding his family in the wild is a once-in-a-lifetime experience.

Of East Africa's thousand or so surviving mountain gorillas, perhaps a quarter live in this Virunga Mountains park. With only a dozen named families habituated to tourist groups, though, bagging a sought-after permit in the main June–September dry season can be a bunfight – you need to book months in advance. But there's another window of opportunity: December marks the start of another, rather less consistently dry patch after the so-called 'short rains'. Squeeze in a visit before Christmas – which heralds another busy spell – and you might snag discounts on lodges, tours and even those all-important gorilla-tracking spots, more easily obtained outside peak season. True, trails may be muddy and nights cool, but with lower costs and thinner crowds, it's a worthwhile payoff.

And Rwanda's no one-trick pony (or primate). Elsewhere, you can spy chimpanzees, monkeys and the 'Big Five' animals, as well as an array of dazzling birdlife.

Left: Mountain gorilla family, Volcanoes National Park **Opposite:** Lake Kivu

EXPERIENCES

ENJOY A FAMILY GATHERING: Meet mountain gorillas in Volcanoes National Park – sparing time to search for golden monkeys, too.

SPOT FIVE ALIVE: Safari through Akagera National Park to seek the Big Five (lion, leopard, buffalo, rhino and elephant), keeping binoculars handy to admire the spectacular birdlife.

JOIN A PRIMATE PARTY: Track chimpanzees and spot grey-cheeked mangabey, Ruwenzori colobus and L'Hoest's monkeys among the mahogany trees and giant ferns of Nyungwe Forest National Park.

SPLASH OUT: Kayak or swim in the clear, fresh waters of Lake Kivu, a worthy detour en route between Volcanoes and Nyungwe Forest National Parks.

NEED TO KNOW

At the time of writing, the standard fee for gorilla-tracking permits in Rwanda is US$1500 per person – but discounts of 30% are available in low season (November–May) for those also booking at least two nights plus an activity in Akagera or Nyungwe Forest National Parks (either two nights in one park, or one in each), bringing the cost down to $1050.

Uzbekistan

NOVEMBER–FEBRUARY

COLD BUT CROWD-LESS

● From around 100 BCE to the 15th century, the Silk Roads stretched for some 6500km (4000 miles) across Asia. Today, arguably the finest remnants of these epic trade routes are in Uzbekistan. That's no secret – it's easily the most visited of the Central Asian republics, especially popular in the spring and autumn. So, to avoid the crowds, plan a winter trip. Caveat: it will be pretty chilly, with lows possibly dipping to just below zero. On the plus side, crisp, blue, cloud-free skies provide the most photogenic backdrop for the exquisitely tiled domes, timeless *madrassas* (Islamic schools) and soaring minarets of the ancient cities. Wrap up warm and you'll be fine.

This is the time to focus on the cultural highlights of Tashkent, Samarkand, Bukhara and Khiva. In these historic hubs, almost everything remains open. Also, the fastest trains between them – speedy Afrosiyob locos – are easier to book outside high season, when tour groups tend to snaffle seats far in advance; enjoy window-seat views of snowcapped mountains and admire the staff in their winter uniforms, complete with fur hats.

Rich and hearty (and meaty), Uzbek food is well-suited to winter wandering, too. Seek out pots of *plov* (pilau, the national dish), warming *laghman* or *shurpa* soups, and *manti* (dumplings).

EXPERIENCES

SEE SAMARKAND: The city's UNESCO-listed treasures include *madrassa*-flanked Registan square; don't miss it lit up at night.

GO SHOPPING: Buy everything from bread and spices to *chapan* (traditional quilted cloaks) at Tashkent's domed Chorsu Bazaar.

TIME-TRAVEL: Wandering Bukhara's UNESCO-listed Old Town, crammed with mosques, workshops, cafes and caravanserais, feels like hopping back centuries.

STAY IN THE ITCHAN KALA: Khiva's walled 'inner city' is like an open-air museum; some of the old buildings have been turned into boutique hotels, so you can wake up amid the atmospheric alleyways.

NEED TO KNOW

Modern, high-speed trains link Tashkent, Samarkand and Bukhara, with slower services continuing to Khiva. Tashkent–Samarkand Afrosiyob trains take 2½ hours, Tashkent–Bukhara just over four hours. Soviet-era trains are slower (Tashkent–Bukhara is eight hours); some have sleeper cars. English isn't widely spoken; learn a few Uzbek words and know the name of your destination in both Latin and Russian-style Cyrillic script.

Left, from top: Itchan Kala carpet weaver, Khiva; Chorsu Bazaar, Tashkent **Opposite:** Gur-e-Amir Mausoleum, Samarkand

Honshū, Japan

DECEMBER–FEBRUARY

WINTER WONDERLAND

● Don't let winter on Japan's largest island give you cold feet. This is a dream time to tackle its historic hiking trails.

With pilgrimages booming worldwide, boots on Japan's ancient paths have multiplied, especially in spring and autumn. Good news: the walking world hasn't yet cottoned on that these routes aren't merely accessible in winter – they're gorgeous and near-empty now, when snowfall can render them even more magical. Same goes for other attractions: Mt Fuji's pristine cone is more dreamlike, and the 'golden pavilion' of Kyoto's Kinkaku-ji temple more enchanting under a dusting of white powder – plus, you're much more likely to capture a photographic masterpiece without being elbowed by selfie-snappers in this quietest season.

Not that snow's inevitable. In fact, swathes of Honshū see more blue skies and much less precipitation of any kind in winter. The Kumano Kodō – one of the country's most popular pilgrimages, traced by devotees for over 1000 years – winds through the Kii Peninsula, a region that rarely dips below freezing. Accommodation prices do take a dip in December, though – and so should you, warming up in one of the natural *onsen* (hot springs). Try digging your own hot bath in the riverbed at Sennin-buro – possible only in winter.

EXPERIENCES

TRAMP EMPTY TRAILS: Pick a route, from easy day-hikes like the 8km (5-mile) Magome–Tsumago section of the Edo-era Nakasendō to a multiday Kumano Kodō pilgrimage.

SAVOUR STEAMING DISHES: Cosy up with a simmering bowl of *nabe* hotpot and warm saké slurped and sipped at a *kotatsu* (heated table).

SEE SNOW MONKEYS: Meet the Japanese macaques soaking in the thermal pools at Jigoku-dani, in Jōshin'etsu-kōgen National Park near Nagano.

EXPLORE KYOTO: Roam old streets lined with wooden *machiya* townhouses, admire magnificent 17th-century castle Nijō-jō, tour temples and sip matcha tea.

NEED TO KNOW

Though the early weeks of December are quiet, and Christmas isn't a major event, things ramp up towards New Year. This is a much bigger deal, celebrated with *bōnenkai* (year-end parties), illuminations and visits to shrines. Ryokan (traditional inns) with their own *onsen* can be in high demand around that time, too, so book ahead.

Left, from top: Kumano Kodō trail; Kinkaku-ji, Kyoto **Opposite:** Snow monkey at Jigoku-dani, Jōshin'etsu-kōgen National Park

NOVEMBER–FEBRUARY

SNOW-WHITE WONDERS

Saxony, Germany

● Like Christmas markets? You'll love the Saxon capital, Dresden. The seasonal bazaar filling the city's Altmarkt (Old Market Square) is reputedly Germany's oldest, first held nearly 600 years ago and now awash with the scents of gluhwein, wurst and roasted almonds. A quieter festive affair worth seeking out is the historic-themed Romantic Market. Away from the markets, Dresden is at its peaceful best outside the May–October peak. True, temperatures hover just above freezing, but you can warm up in the city's astonishing museums, many only lately restored after wartime devastation. Discover the extravagant pleasure-gardens-palace complex of the Zwinger; spectacular art at the Albertinum, set in a former arsenal; and the Residenzschloss (Royal Palace), featuring the opulent treasures of the Green Vault.

More jewels of a geological type lie upstream along the Elbe River, just a half-hour train ride from Dresden: the sandstone mountain region dubbed 'Saxon Switzerland' by 18th-century painters. In summer, parts of this forested wonderland – Bastei Bridge, for example – can be swarming with selfie-snapping tourists. But in winter, you can have its bizarrely sculpted rock outcrops pretty much to yourself; explore on foot along the 116km-long (72-mile) Malerweg (Painters' Path), visiting spots immortalised by Romantic artists such as Caspar David Friedrich.

Left, from top: Zwinger, Dresden; Bastei Bridge **Opposite:** Altmarkt Christmas market, Dresden

EXPERIENCES

ADMIRE OLD GOLD: Roam the jewels of Dresden's Altstadt (Old Town), including restored gems such as the wedding-cake Frauenkirche, Residenzschloss and Zwinger, and make time to discover the artsy Kunsthofpassage in the Neustadt (New Town).

PACE INTO THE PICTURE: Tramp the trails of the Malerweg between and up the curious rock formations of 'Saxon Switzerland' (officially the Elbe Sandstone Mountains).

TAKE YOUR (VINE) TIME: Savour fine drops produced by vineyards along the Saxon Wine Route; some wineries, such as Schloss Wackerbarth, are lit up with enchanting decorations in winter.

NEED TO KNOW

Though the Malerweg as a whole is open year-round, some stretches can be sketchy in snow or ice; wear study footwear and consider hiring *grödel* (antislip spikes) from the Tourist Service centre in Bad Schandau. Forestry work is sometimes undertaken in winter, too – closures and diversions are advised online *(saechsische-schweiz.de)*. Some accommodation and other facilities close between January and March, too.

Ireland

DECEMBER

LIGHT IN THE DARK

● To be sure, it'll be cold, dark and damp. But Ireland exudes an otherworldly magic in December. This is a land steeped in storytelling and spirituality, with Neolithic sites that predate Egypt's pyramids. The most extraordinary is Brú na Bóinne (Boyne Valley tombs), a UNESCO-listed burial complex in County Meath where, on the winter solstice, sunlight pierces the passage of the site's Newgrange tomb to illuminate the inner chamber. Tickets to be inside for this annual awakening are difficult to score (entry is decided via lottery), but regardless, it's an atmospheric time to explore Ireland's sacred past, with far fewer tourists around.

For instance, take the Hill of Tara: winter's hush enhances the mood of this ancient ceremonial mound, from where Ireland's High Kings once ruled. Although the visitor centre closes for the season, the sacred landscape is free to access year-round, and looks especially bewitching adorned with a sparkling cloak of frost.

And yes, while days are short, there's always a warm welcome in the pub. Whether you've been roaming monastery ruins, puzzling over ancient stone circles or watching surfers ride huge winter swells from wind-whipped clifftops, Irish drinking holes lure with glowing hearths, trad music and a whiskey or two.

Left: Kytelers Inn, Kilkenny. **Opposite:** Brú na Bóinne, County Meath

EXPERIENCES

FEEL FESTIVE: Christmas markets add cheer to dark days; Galway's is huge, complete with stalls, beer tents and a Ferris wheel.

ENJOY THE CRAIC: The cobbled lanes of towns such as Kilkenny and Limerick are good places to seek out cosy bars; or try Doolin, capital of traditional Irish music.

SEEK ANCIENT SITES: Explore Loughcrew megalithic cemetery in Meath, where passage tombs date to 3000 BCE.

CATCH A BREAK: Watch big-wave riders at Mullaghmore Head in Sligo, or take a surf course at more sheltered spots, such as Ballybunion in Kerry.

NEED TO KNOW

A tot of Irish whiskey offers a quick way to warm up. Ireland claims to have invented the spirit around 1000 years ago, and makes it differently from its Scottish equivalent, usually distilling it thrice, not twice. It's currently enjoying a revival, with 40-plus distilleries thriving across the country, many offering tours. Try Jameson, which has distilleries in both Dublin and Cork.

Côte d'Azur, France

NOVEMBER–FEBRUARY

ROYAL WINTER

● Queen Victoria loved overwintering on the French Riviera. And if it was good enough for the redoubtable British monarch back then, it's good enough for us riffraff today. Back in the 19th century, this was peak season in the resorts along this dazzling Mediterranean shore, from Menton to St-Tropez. They were lauded for their comparatively mild climates – December temperatures hover at 10°–14°C (50°–57°F) – as well as their healthy, salt-spritzed air and the luminous light that attracted painters, notably Chagall, Picasso and Matisse.

These days it's summer that draws the crowds. So if you choose to come offseason (which, confusingly, used to be on-season), you'll have the run of the place. The twisty, scenic coast roads will be far quieter, the hotels much cheaper. Lively, likeable Nice hosts a Village de Noël (Christmas Village) and Monaco puts on a big festive market, both of which draw December visitors; even so, there's still plenty of space to inhale that revivifying sea breeze.

The cool weather is perfect for walking, too. Stroll along the various *sentiers du littoral* (paths linking coastal villages), or hike inland: the stiff climb to the hilltop village of Èze via the Chemin de Nietzsche will certainly warm you up.

EXPERIENCES

APPRECIATE ART: Museums dedicated to Picasso in Antibes, Matisse in Nice and Jean Cocteau in Menton are all good options for cooler days, and are open year-round.

ISLAND-HOP: Ferries run from Cannes to the Îles de Lérins: Ste-Marguerite offers *Man in the Iron Mask* intrigue (he was imprisoned here); minuscule Île St-Honorat is a working monastery.

COLD-WATER DIP: At 15°C-ish (59°F), the sea isn't *that* chilly; join or watch the mid-December Nice Christmas swim.

LOOK UP: Winter skies tend to be clearer – perfect for stargazing or a visit to Observatoire de la Côte d'Azur near Nice.

NEED TO KNOW

January and February are the coldest months on the French Riviera, but still enticing times to visit. Mimosa trees burst into golden bloom January to March; see and smell them driving the 130km (81-mile) Route du Mimosa through the Mandelieu-La Napoule region. In February, Nice hosts a humongous Carnival, while Menton's Fête du Citron is a two-week orange-and-lemon extravaganza.

Left, from top: Menton; Île St-Honorat **Opposite:** Jardin Exotique d'Èze

Photo Credits

Cover: Zhan Xunchao/Shutterstock; **Flap:** NewJadsada/Shutterstock, Igor Tichonow/Getty Images; **Back Cover:** D.Bond/Shutterstock; **2:** ermess/Shutterstock; **6:** Tiago Fialho/Shutterstock; **7:** chrisontour84/Shutterstock; **8:** Pete Seaward for Lonely Planet; **10:** EyesWideOpen/Getty Images; **12:** JMS Splash Photography/Shutterstock; **13:** Zaruba Ondrej/Shutterstock; **14:** Russ Nordstrand/500px; **15(l):** Shuttericon/Shutterstock; **15(r):** Wei Hao Ho/Getty Images; **16:** Mikadun/Shutterstock; **17(l):** Frank Lambert/Shutterstock; **17(r):** Lovethief Photography/Getty Images; **18:** Cristian M Balate/Shutterstock; **19(l):** DSLR/Shutterstock; **19(r):** Nomad Pixel/Shutterstock; **20:** bonchan/Getty Images; **21:** Cyprien Charra/Shutterstock; **22:** Lukas Kovarik/Shutterstock; **23(l):** Esteban Alejandro/Shutterstock; **23(r):** AndamanSE/Getty Images; **24:** Joseph Polo/Shutterstock; **25(l):** EyesWideOpen/Getty Images; **25(r):** Guy Wilkinson/Shutterstock; **26:** f11photo/Shutterstock; **27(l):** Robert Davis/Alamy; **27(r):** Joshua Resnick/Shutterstock; **28:** GEORGE STAMATIS/Shutterstock; **30:** imageBROKER.com/Alamy; **31:** Robert Peternel/500px; **32:** Visual Collective/Shutterstock; **33(l):** zstock/Shutterstock; **33(r):** SOPA Images/Getty Images; **34:** f8grapher/Getty Images; **35(l):** Ivo Antonie de Rooij/Shutterstock; **35(r):** Theastock/Shutterstock; **36:** Andrea Pistolesi/Getty Images; **37:** Philip Reeve/Shutterstock; **38:** OPIS Zagreb/Shutterstock; **39(l):** nejdetduzen/Getty Images; **39(r):** Toa55/Shutterstock; **40:** Laura G.Robe/Shutterstock; **41(l):** Lucy.Brown/Shutterstock; **41(r):** Matteo Colombo/Getty Images; **42:** Mark Blinch/Getty Images; **43:** Ric Jacyno/Shutterstock; **44:** Trong Nguyen/Shutterstock; **45(l):** Kushal Bose/Shutterstock; **45(r):** stock_photo_world/Shutterstock; **46:** Sabine Hortebusch/Shutterstock; **48:** Rod //Getty Images; **49:** Jane Rix/Shutterstock; **50:** Frank Günther/Getty Images; **51(l):** MZPHOTO.CZ/Shutterstock; **51(r):** NicoElNino/iStock; **52:** Angelo Cavalli/Getty Images; **53(l):** s_jakkarin/Shutterstock; **53(r):** lakkana savaksuriyawong/Shutterstock; **54:** soft_light/Shutterstock; **55(l):** DivelvanovShutterstock; **55(r):** Oscar Espinosa/Shutterstock; **56:** Vaclav Sonnek/Shutterstock; **57(l):** Bruno Coelho/Alamy; **57(r):** Clare Hargreaves/Alamy; **58:** Unai Huizi Photography/Shutterstock; **59(l):** Ingólfur Bjargmundsson/Getty Images; **59(r):** Petr Klabal/Shutterstock; **60:** Andrei Molchan/Shutterstock; **61:** BERK OZDEMIR/Shutterstock; **62:** Galyna Andrushko/Shutterstock; **63(l):** Sangkhom Hungkhunthod/Shutterstock; **63(r):** Danita Delimont/Shutterstock; **64:** Vpommeyrol/Getty Images; **66:** Ariadne Van Zandbergen/Alamy; **67(l):** Subodh Agnihotri/Getty Images; **67(r):** AYOTOGRAPHY/Getty Images; **68:** Paul Cameron Allen/Shutterstock; **69:** f9photos/Getty Images; **70:** AhXiong/Shutterstock; **71(l):** Pete Seaward for Lonely Planet; **71(r):** SvetlanaSF/Shutterstock; **72:** VTT Studio/Shutterstock; **73(l):** Sean Hsu/Shutterstock; **73(r):** ThePonAek/Shutterstock; **74:** Adwo/Shutterstock; **75(l):** Nicram Sabod/Shutterstock; **75(r):** cktravels.com/Shutterstock; **76:** Maridav/Shutterstock; **77:** Jon Ruiz Ortiz/Shutterstock; **78:** Mac Tv Films/Shutterstock; **79(l):** Ikonya/Shutterstock; **79(r):** Marcos Campos/Shutterstock; **80:** Dee Carpenter Originals/Shutterstock; **81(l):** Andrew Peacock/Getty Images; **81(r):** Anton_Ivanov/Shutterstock; **82:** KenWiedemann/Getty Images; **83(l):** Eli De Faria for Lonely Planet; **83(r):** The Roaming Dad/Shutterstock; **84:** Julieta Gonzalez Checchin/Shutterstock; **86:** Fabio Lamanna/Shutterstock; **87(l):** Ward Poppe/Shutterstock; **87(r):** DaweArt/Shutterstock; **88:** Faiz Zaki/Shutterstock; **89(l):** B_BEUM/Shutterstock; **89(r):** Sergey Uryadnikov/Shutterstock; **90:** Mary Hitselberger/Shutterstock; **91:** xbrchx/Shutterstock; **92:** Ikunl/Shutterstock; **93(l):** Jon Chica/Shutterstock; **93(r):** pinnee.com/Getty Images; **94:** foto-select/Shutterstock; **95(l):** saiko3p/Shutterstock; **95(r):** Westend61/Getty Images; **96:** gadag/Shutterstock; **97(l):** Guste L/Shutterstock; **97(r):** Martins Vanags/Shutterstock; **98:** Alexandree/Shutterstock; **99(l):** Milton Rodriguez/Shutterstock; **99(r):** Nancy Hajjar/Shutterstock; **100:** Tec Petaja for Lonely Planet; **101:** Steve Heap/Shutterstock; **102:** Scott Heaney/Shutterstock; **103(l):** Justek16/Shutterstock; **103(r):** zixian/Shutterstock; **104:** Aaron. Weatherston/Shutterstock; **106:** Diego Fiore/Shutterstock; **107(l):** Don Mammoser/Shutterstock; **107(r):** Catherine Sutherland for Lonely Planet; **108:** Curioso/Shutterstock; **109:** kasakphoto/Shutterstock; **110:** zetter/Getty Images; **111(l):** Oliver Strewe/Getty Images; **111(r):** Greg Balfour Evans/Alamy; **112:** Christian Wittmann/Shutterstock; **113(l):** Hyserb/Shutterstock; **113(r):** ollirg/Shutterstock; **114:** Kirk Fisher/Shutterstock; **115(l):** Mirjam Claus/Shutterstock; **115(r):** dnaveh/Shutterstock; **116:** Maurizio De Mattei/Shutterstock; **117(l):** rhfletcher/Shutterstock; **117(r):** Mark Read for Lonely Planet; **118:** M Swiet Productions/Getty Images; **119(l):** YuziS/Shutterstock; **119(r):** 365 Focus Photography/Shutterstock; **120:** thinair28/Getty Images; **121(l):** Jason Kolenda/Shutterstock; **121(r):** Andrew Peacock/Getty Images; **122:** D.Bond/Shutterstock; **124:** Curioso.Photography/Shutterstock; **125(l):** Elena Ska/Shutterstock; **125(r):** Igor Tichonow/Shutterstock; **126:** Tuul and Bruno Morandi/Getty Images; **127:** pilesasmiles/Getty Images; **128:** Ramesh Thadani/Getty Images; **129(l):** Uwe Bergwitz/Shutterstock; **129(r):** Paulo Jr/Shutterstock; **130:** Yashrib/Getty Images; **131(l):** Andrei Armiagov/Shutterstock; **131(r):** Vincenzo Caricato/Shutterstock; **132:** Pav-Pro Photography Ltd/Shutterstock; **133(l):** Jakub Maculewicz/Shutterstock; **133(r):** wintawatwinwin/Shutterstock; **134:** JohannesS/Shutterstock; **135:** fokke baarssen/Shutterstock; **136:** Alex Segre/Shutterstock; **137(l):** Joerg Steber/Shutterstock; **137(r):** Guillermo Ossa/Shutterstock; **138:** Paul Souders/Getty Images; **139(l):** chbaum/Shutterstock; **139(r):** Agami Photo Agency/Shutterstock; **140:** CRS PHOTO/Shutterstock; **142:** Alexandre G. ROSA/Shutterstock; **143(l):** Joseph Sohm/Shutterstock; **143(r):** Neissl/Shutterstock; **144:** Marcin Szymczak/Shutterstock; **145:** Santhosh kumar sundaresan/Shutterstock; **146:** Dmitry Rukhlenko/Shutterstock; **147(l):** Sahana M S/Shutterstock; **147(r):** Nate Hovee/Shutterstock; **148:** Adwo/Shutterstock; **149(l):** Andrea Izzotti/Shutterstock; **149(r):** inavanhateren/Shutterstock; **150:** Hemis/Alamy; **151(l):** Peter Krocka/Shutterstock; **151(r):** R Gombarik/Shutterstock; **152:** stoyanh/Shutterstock; **153(l):** rh2010/Adobestock; **153(r):** Dennis van de Water/Shutterstock; **154:** smilephotoarg/Shutterstock; **155(l):** Sobrevolando Patagonia/Shutterstock; **155(r):** Matt Munro for Lonely Planet; **156:** Katia Titova/Shutterstock; **158:** Mark R Croucher/Shutterstock; **159(l):** Richard Sharrocks/Getty Images; **159(r):** Gareth Bogdanoff/500px; **160:** Sergii Figurnyi/Shutterstock; **161:** Andras Jancsik/Getty Images; **162:** RiadSeif/Shutterstock; **163(l):** Marieke Kramer/Shutterstock; **163(r):** Katiekk/Shutterstock; **164:** EAGiven/Getty Images; **165(l):** lepir/Shutterstock; **165(r):** Agent Wolf/Shutterstock; **166:** blue-sea.cz/Shutterstock; **167(l):** byvalet/Shutterstock; **167(r):** Westend61/Getty Images; **168:** Mikhail Varentsov/Shutterstock; **169:** Martin Ruegner/Getty Images; **170:** Uhryn Larysa/Shutterstock; **171(l&r):** Justin Foulkes for Lonely Planet; **172:** StDavit/Shutterstock; **173(l):** Mike Ilchenko/Shutterstock; **173(r):** AlexelA/Shutterstock; **174:** yhelfman/Shutterstock; **175(l):** Karel Stipek/Shutterstock; **175(r):** Nikolay Tsuguliev/Getty Images; **176:** cworthy/Shutterstock; **177:** J Duquette/Shutterstock; **177:** Foodgraphy39/Shutterstock; **178:** cpaulfell/Shutterstock; **180:** Kadagan/Shutterstock; **181(l):** Max shen/Getty Images; **181(r):** Ender BAYINDIR/Shutterstock; **182:** dibrova/Shutterstock; **183(l):** proslgn/Shutterstock; **183(r):** Justin Foulkes for Lonely Planet; **184:** CravenA/Shutterstock; **185(l):** Prawat Thananithaporn/Shutterstock; **185(r):** structuresxx/Shutterstock; **186:** Peter Adams/Getty Images; **187:** Natthawat/Getty Images; **188:** Poike/Getty Images; **189(l):** Mazur Travel/Shutterstock; **189(r):** PNIKOL/Shutterstock; **190:** James Gregory Photography/Shutterstock; **191(l):** Jacinto Marabel Romo/Shutterstock; **191(r):** Gonzalo Azumendi/Getty Images; **192:** Tupungato/Shutterstock; **193(l):** Steve Allen/Getty Images;**193(r):** John Maier Jr for Lonely Planet; **194:** All Canada Photos/Alamy; **195:** Nalidsa/Shutterstock; **196:** Thomas Janisch/Getty Images; **197(l):** Matt Elliott/Shutterstock; **197(r):** barmalini/Shutterstock; **198:** Sean Newbery/Shutterstock; **200:** Bossa Art/Shutterstock; **201(l):** dennisvdw/Getty Images; **201(r):** Sergey Didenko/Shutterstock; **202:** Jonathan Gregson for Lonely Planet; **203(l):** StanislavBeloglazov/Shutterstock; **203(r):** Steve Adams/Getty Images; **204:** DrHao/Shutterstock; **205:** Seung Ha Kim/Shutterstock; **206:** NS Photograph/Shutterstock; **207(l):** topten22photo/Shutterstock; **207(r):** Viktoriya Krayn/Shutterstock; **208:** Tatiana_kashko_photo/Shutterstock; **209(l):** Efired/Shutterstock; **209(r):** Meiqianbao/Shutterstock; **210:** Westend61/Getty Images; **211(l):** trabantos/Shutterstock; **211(r):** Alberto Fornasari/Shutterstock; **212:** Kirk Fisher/Shutterstock; **213(l):** Beketoff/Shutterstock; **213(r):** Matt Munro for Lonely Planet; **214:** Wirestock Creators/Shutterstock; **215:** Viacheslav Lopatin/Shutterstock; **216:** ElOjoTorpe/Getty Images; **217(l):** RPBaiao/Shutterstock; **217(r):** Sergi Reboredo/Alamy; **218:** Gary Yeowell/Getty Images; **220:** ProPIC/Getty Images; **221(l):** Checco2/Shutterstock; **221(r):** yalcins/Shutterstock; **222:** LMspencer/Shutterstock; **223:** Mary Ann McDonald/Shutterstock; **224:** NICOLA MESSANA PHOTOS/Shutterstock; **225(l):** Mlenny/Getty Images; **225(r):** becauz gao/Shutterstock; **226:** Photos by Tai GinDa/Getty Images; **227(l):** Club4traveler/Shutterstock; **227(r):** LLUCO/Shutterstock; **228:** Tatiana Diuvbanova/Shutterstock; **229(l&r):** Elizaveta Kovaleva for Lonely Planet; **230:** MNStudio/Shutterstock; **231:** littlenySTOCK/Shutterstock; **232:** berm_teerawat/Shutterstock; **233(l):** Taljat David/Shutterstock; **233(r):** GLF Media/Shutterstock; **235:** Gonzalo Buzonni/Shutterstock;

Castelo dos Mouros, Sintra, Portugal

Index

A

B

C

Offseason
Project Editors Becca Hunt, Robin Barton
Publishing Director Piers Pickard
Editorial Director Becca Hunt
Art Director Emily Dubin
Print Production Nigel Longuet

September 2026
Published by Lonely Planet Global Limited
CRN: 554153
ISBN: 9781837587605

10 9 8 7 6 5 4 3 2 1
Printed in Malaysia

STAY IN TOUCH
lonelyplanet.com/contact

Lonely Planet Office:
IRELAND
Digital Depot, Roe Lane (off Thomas St),
Digital Hub, Dublin 8, D08 TCV4, Ireland
(EU authorised representative)

MIX
Paper | Supporting responsible forestry
FSC www.fsc.org
FSC™ C021741

Paper in this book is certified against the Forest Stewardship Council™ standards. FSC™ promotes environmentally responsible, socially beneficial and economically viable management of the world's forests.